The Book of
HOUSES

Triune Books

The Book of
HOUSES

Geoffrey Hindley

The publishers gratefully acknowledge the following who have supplied the illustrations for this book:
J. Allan Cash, London 14t, 16t, 24b, 26t, 36b, 37t, 39b, 39t, 52, 54t, 56t, 58t, 58c, 65t, 68, 69t, 69b, 72b, 80t, 81t, 100b, 101; American Museum in Bath 135b; Ashmolean Museum, Oxford 8t, 9t, b, 10t, b, 44t; Barnaby's Picture Library, London 131, 138t; Bavaria–Verlag 12, 28tl, 28bl, 29bl, 29br, 40, 102, 114b, 119tl, 128b; Stefan Buzas, London 30b, 95; Cement and Concrete Association, London 130tr; Cooper–Bridgeman Library, London 66; Trewin Copplestone, London 142b; Country Life, London 74, 79tl, tr; Courtauld Institute of Art, London 38l, 38br, 60; Dutch Society of Sciences, Haarlem 34r; John R. Freeman, London 129tr; Photographic Giraudon, Paris 18, 19; Glasgow University Art Collection 48t; Susan Griggs, London 142t; Hamlyn Group, London 6t, 17t, 20c, 32, 36t, 77t, 82tr, 83tr, 84, 90t, 122, 126t, 130b, 141t, 143t; Hampshire County Museum Service 49t; Robert Harding Associates, London 143b; Lucien Hervé, Paris 7t, b, 1, 43t, b, 119tr, 119b, 131b; India Office Library and Records, London 129br, 130l; Philip Johnson, New York 144t, b; Keele University Library 49b; A. F. Kersting, London 1, 17b, 20b, 23b, 42, 53, 56b, 62, 63b, 64t, 65b, 75, 76, 80b, 83tl, 87, 112; Paolo Koch, Zollikon 120, 121tr, 121br, 123t, 124t, b, 125t, b, 126b; Eric Lyons, Cunningham and Partners, London 166; Musée National du Château de Malmaison 88; Mansell Collection, London 8, 30t, 44b, 118b; Mitchell Beazley Ltd., London 55t; National Gallery, London 11, 38l; National Gallery, Washington DC., Gift of Edgar and Bernice Garbisch 14b; National Monuments Record, London 15, 48b, 55b; National Trust, London 13, 59b, 81b, 82tl, 85; Picturepoint, London 26, 67t, b, 78, 79, 103, 139; RIBA, London 82b, 138b, 141b; Scala, Florence 22t, 98t, 99t; Science Museum, London 58b; Spectrum Colour Library, London 25t, 27t, b, 28b, 31b, 33t, b, 34l, 37b, 51, 70, 98b, 134, 135t; Dr. Franz Stoedtner, Dusseldorf 118t; Thames and Hudson, Ltd., London 97b; Agence TOP, Paris 106, 107, 108b, 110, 111; Victoria and Albert Museum, London 23tr; Wallace Collection, London 23tl; Wayland Ltd, London 18b, 21, 22b, 24t, 31t, 46t, 46b, 47t, 47b, 50t, b; Weidenfeld and Nicolson Ltd, London 3, 35, 59t, 61, 64b, 70t, 71, 72t, 73, 77b, 86t, 86b, 90b, 91, 92t, 93, 94, 96t, 96b, 97t, 99b, 100t, 102t, 104, 105, 108t, 113l, 113r, 113b, 114t, 115t, 115b, 116, 117t, 117bl, 117br, 127, 128t, 132, 136t, 136b, 137b, 139t; Woburn Abbey Park 57t.

ISBN 0 85674 025 X
Published by
Triune Books, London, England
© Trewin Copplestone Publishing Ltd 1973
Printed in Spain by
Printer Industria Gráfica SA, Tuset 19, Barcelona
San Vicente dels Horts
Depósito legal B 18974–1973
Mohn Gordon Ltd, London

Page 1 The remarkable rococo chinoiserie decorations around the door in the Chinese Room, Claydon, which were executed by the local craftsman, Luke Lightfoot.

Page 3 The rustic kitchen complete with pine furniture and open fireplace at Monticello, near Charlottesville, Va., the home of Thomas Jefferson.

Contents

Machines for Living In

'A machine for living in'; it is certainly a challenging definition of a house. The quotation is generally attributed to the Swiss-born architect, Le Corbusier, though he has disclaimed authorship. Even so, it is obviously an architect's phrase intended to shock people into a complete rethink of what they expect of a house. Is it merely a form of convenient accommodation or is it something more? So we start this book with an investigation of some of the functions of the house throughout history and some of the qualities of domestic life in the past.

The house has never been merely a shelter. The cave paintings of pre-historic man show us that when men settle in even the most primitive form of shelter, it becomes something more than that. A house is a permanent dwelling, often inhabited by the same family and its descendants over a long period of time. We shall be seeing a number of 'machines for living in' in this book; they range from the grandiose to the humble, but they have this in common that they all have to accommodate that variable and awkward commodity, human nature.

Shortly after the Second World War, Le Corbusier received a commission from the French Ministry of Reconstruction to build a block of flats in Marseilles in southern France, intended to house 1500 people. The result was a building which some feel revolutionized the direction of modern architecture. This is partly because of the exciting way in which the architect handled the technical problems posed by post-war shortages both in materials and skilled labour. The genius of Le Corbusier was able to create architectural poetry in the textured surfaces he got from rough and often clumsily cast concrete.

For us the social concept of the Unité d'Habitation ('Dwelling Unit'), is even more interesting. The whole building rests on massive pillars. Le Corbusier, in the 1940s far ahead of the current environmental fashion, regarded land as a scarce resource, so at Marseilles children play in the open air and drivers park their cars under a vertical township. For, besides the residential flats, stacked 'like bottles in a rack', there is also a huge shopping precinct half way up the building and even a hotel. On the roof there is a gymnasium and swimming pool as the architect aimed to provide all the services of a town in his Unité.

Le Corbusier was also determined to give the low income families for whom the place was designed, the sense of spacious living and grandeur found in the lofty rooms of a mansion. Each flat has a two-storeyed living room with a gallery round it at first floor level for the bed. Stretching back from it through the width of the building were long narrow second bedroom, kitchen and bathroom. These dwellings, shaped like an 'L' on its back overlapped one another so that two flats took up three storeys. The idea was brilliant and enlightened, but for a large family, where those sleeping in the living room gallery are bound to be disturbed if others want to sit up late, there are obvious practical disadvantages. The same sort

The Swiss-born architect Le Corbusier built his Unité d'Habitation at Marseilles, France, to provide low cost housing for about 1500 people. Because he regarded land as a scarce resource he raised the building on pillars, called 'pilotis'. The roof, with its sensational view of the neighbouring mountains, was used to the full, with play areas for children and sports facilities. *Below right* The interior of a flat by Le Corbusier.

of thing has been found in many other flats.

'Housing' and 'accommodation' are the words we tend to use today instead of 'house'. People have to be put somewhere and the answer is often these high rise flats to make the maximum use of land and materials. But living at great heights can be psychologically disturbing while the fact that children may have to go the whole height of the building to reach their playgrounds and that the entrances to the dwelling units are on long and usually dark corridors, breaks up the sense of community that is to be found in a conventional city street of family houses. For many people a house of their own is the ideal. A house is not just a form of accommodation, it is something more.

In every civilisation it is the great houses that have set the fashions which others have followed where they can. In the West, the Roman villa was for centuries the ideal of the house for the rich and powerful. 'My dear Gallus, you may wonder why my Laurentine place is such a joy to me, but once you realise the attractions of the house itself, the amenities of its situation, and its extensive seafront, you will have your answer.' The writer is Pliny the Younger and in the letter that follows he sets out the beauties of the ideal country place near Rome in about the year AD 100. It was the city man's dream, only seventeen miles from the capital so it was possible to do a full day's work and ride back in time for dinner.

The main dining room was, in Pliny's view, 'really rather fine.' It ran out towards the sea so that when the wind was in the right direction light plumes of spray came into the terrace; when the weather was colder or rougher one simply had to close the folding glass doors so as to enjoy the luxury of a modern waterside restaurant. Leading off from the dining room was a suite of bedrooms and a library set so that the rays of the morning and evening sun streamed in on them; behind them were the rooms of the slaves and freedmen. Along the sea-front from the dining room was the ball court and the heated swimming pool, 'much admired and from which the swimmers can see the sea.' On the land side was a small dining room overlooking a quiet garden and a pergola for vines where the soil was soft and gentle even to bare feet; in the corner between this and the dining room was the well stocked kitchen garden. The far side of the vine garden was bounded by an arcade with windows looking out onto the sea, which led out to the suite of rooms that Pliny built onto the house as his personal retreat. Here was a sun room facing the terrace on one side and the sea on the other with next to it a beautiful alcove divided from the sun room by glass partitions and curtains which could be drawn to make a single charming room. The letter is so detailed that a modern scholar has been able to build a scale model of Pliny's place in the country.

The description also contains a number of themes that will recur in this book. The wealthy Roman certainly did not look on his house as a machine for living in. Pliny was a busy imperial administrator and Laurentia provided for him a peaceful retreat from the cares of the city. The city dweller's yearning for the countryside is as old as civilisation. Excavation has revealed handsome country villas on the fringes of ancient

The reconstructed model of Pliny's villa, was built up from a description in one of his letters. Guests play in the ball court and bathe in the sea. In the foreground is the private retreat Pliny built for himself. It was approached through a pergola like the one from the house at Pompeii (*bottom left*). *Bottom right* A ground plan of the model in the Ashmolean Museum, Oxford.

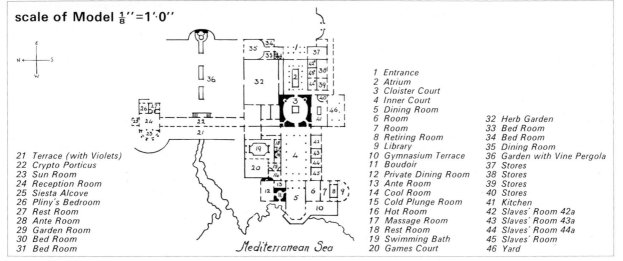

scale of Model ⅛″=1′·0″

1 Entrance
2 Atrium
3 Cloister Court
4 Inner Court
5 Dining Room
6 Room
7 Room
8 Retiring Room
9 Library
10 Gymnasium Terrace
11 Boudoir
12 Private Dining Room
13 Ante Room
14 Cool Room
15 Cold Plunge Room
16 Hot Room
17 Massage Room
18 Rest Room
19 Swimming Bath
20 Games Court

21 Terrace (with Violets)
22 Crypto Porticus
23 Sun Room
24 Reception Room
25 Siesta Alcove
26 Pliny's Bedroom
27 Rest Room
28 Ante Room
29 Garden Room
30 Bed Room
31 Bed Room

32 Herb Garden
33 Bed Room
34 Bed Room
35 Dining Room
36 Garden with Vine Pergola
37 Stores
38 Stores
39 Stores
40 Stores
41 Kitchen
42 Slaves' Room 42a
43 Slaves' Room 43a
44 Slaves' Room 44a
45 Slaves' Room
46 Yard

Mediterranean Sea

Egyptian cities such as Thebes and the learned mandarin class that ran the Chinese empire also longed for rustic retirement. In the second place, Pliny provided himself with a private study, a retreat within the retreat so to speak, to cut him off from the world as far as possible. Thirdly, the place was a large establishment; Pliny stood at the head of a sizeable community which in addition to his family included guests, servants and slaves.

Above The entrance courtyard to Pliny's villa. On one side of the porch there is a store room.
Below The terrace skirts the main dining room and the semi-circular apsed library. Along from the library run the slaves' quarters.

Aristotle was the first political theorist to use the household as a model for the structure of the state. The simile held good for two thousand years. Like Pliny, the Victorian *pater familias* governed his household with an almost autocratic authority and in most cultures the house has been the home of a large and real community, governed like a mini-state. The fourth point we should notice about Pliny's account is the obvious luxury of the villa. It represents a pattern of urbane living that was not to be achieved in Europe for more than a thousand years after the fall of the Roman empire.

To take an example, central heating, which the Romans had developed to a moderately sophisticated degree, was for centuries a lost art. In medieval Europe, the gap between rich and poor was far greater than it is today and the furnishings of their houses naturally reflected the fact. But the actual type of facilities available for both of them were much the same. For both, domestic heating depended on the open fire in the grate and layers of heavy clothing. The Limbourg brothers give a charming insight into the life of peasant and nobleman in the magnificent illuminations they painted for the Duke of Berri's devotional Book of Hours. The peasant and his wife, after a hard day in the fields, have little compunction about dropping their sodden breeches to dry off; the aristocrat enjoys the luxury of an adjustable wicker-work fire screen to protect his face and eyes from stinging smoke and flying sparks. In spite of such elegant refinements it is quite possible that the room of the peasant was the warmer, if only because it was the smaller.

The Duke's dining table is set so that the great men can sit on the long bench with their backs to the fire. The bench is covered with draperies. It is probable that its back is a single rail which would support but would not block off the heat of the fire; it could probably be swung from back to front depending on whether the sitter wanted to face the fire or away from it. Although the Duke is full in front of the fire, he is still heavily robed and is even wearing a fur hat. A tourist visiting the great houses and palaces of Europe sooner or later finds himself asking just how their owners kept these vast places warm. The simple answer is that by and large they did not. These houses were built primarily for display, and comfort simply did not have the overriding priority that we give it in our homes today.

Of course, gentlemen did their best to provide efficient heating in their homes. The Duke of Este asked the great artist Raphael to design a smokeless fireplace, and a whole chapter in one sixteenth century book on architecture deals with fires and chimneys. Houses were sometimes abandoned because fireplaces and flues just did not work at all, but things had to be pretty bad, and people would put up with astonishing conditions. The grandiose palace of Versailles was bitterly criticised by courtiers. The royal mistress, Madame de Maintenon, caustically observed that in winter the royal bedroom was swept by draughts 'like American hurricanes'. Eventually she had a special inner room built which would hold an armchair and a bed. The king's doctor may have given her the idea. Apparently determined to preserve at least his own health in the royal icebox of a palace, he complacently sat in a sedan chair before the fires of its marbled halls. However splendid the luxuries of Europe's great palaces and houses, warmth does not seem to have been one of the important factors.

A detail from a fifteenth century Flemish painting. We look out onto the town square. Two rich merchants are in town on business and a workman is repairing a roof. In the foreground is the arm of a bench; the channel allows the back rail to be moved from front to back to let people face the fire or have their backs to it, without having to move the heavy bench.

During the eighteenth century, matters improved somewhat with the development of an improved enclosed stove. Fine porcelain-tiled room heaters from this period are still to be seen in many of Europe's baroque palaces, while in America Benjamin Franklin, that man of many parts, devised an effective slow-burning domestic grate that was to be perfected and remodelled in the nineteenth century. English ingenuity seems to have been devoted to protection from draughts. 'Wing' chairs with side pieces and then canopies virtually enveloped the sitter, while iron or brass foot warmers filled with glowing coals were provided.

Often bed was the warmest place. The elaborate four-posters so admired today, with heavy curtains and canopies, cut out much of the draught. In addition they offered some privacy in a period when rooms did not have the specialist functions we expect today. When one member of the household had retired to bed, others might use the room for other purposes and it was common for lords and ladies to begin the day's business with a reception held from their beds in a room thronging with servants and petitioners. The French word *levée*, which literally means 'getting up', has become a synonym for a formal reception.

Household sanitation was if anything worse than heating. Various types of water closets, using running streams or artificial means, have been discovered in ancient Crete and Rome, while white-washed rooms for bath and sand-box earth closet have been excavated in comparatively modest Egyptian houses. Even in the European middle ages, public baths were common enough and paintings from the sixteenth century and before show us men and women bathing in deep tubs lined with silks and linen. But around 1700, conditions in even the finest houses were primitive. Chamber pots were emptied into an open canal in the street or the night soil was removed by wagons. Nor was there privacy even in the privy. One courtier had the job of holding the French king's sword while he discussed affairs of state with ministers as he sat on the 'close stool'. Not surprisingly, the royal toilet seat became an important piece of furniture. The fourteenth century French King John II had one covered in painted velvet while Marie Antoinette was charged 3000 livres by a cabinet maker for a commode decorated with bronze mounts and painted with birds.

Those who could afford it generally did try to find a healthy situation for their house. In ancient Athens, revered to day as the birthplace of western intellectual traditions, the citizens took little interest in the refinements of domestic comfort. One visitor commented on the poverty of the houses there as compared with other Greek cities, while another, the great Aristotle who settled there as a teacher, turned his attention to household management as to most other things. On choosing a situation he had this to say: 'for well-being and health, the house should be well ventilated in summer and catch the sun in winter and it should be protected from northerly winds.' Pliny prided himself on his beautiful and healthy coastal site and good air and fine views would seem to be the most important factors governing the choice of a site.

But in other civilisations and at other times the choice has involved very different considerations. In China, it was believed that a house could exert influence for good and evil and to ensure the goodwill of the spirits, diviners and geomancers were called on to advise on the orientation, ground plan and the day on which to begin the building. Sometimes even these precautions were not thought sufficient and many a great house had a screen just behind the main gate to block the way to evil spirits. Among the Yoruba people of West Central Nigeria, the choice of site poses human as well as spiritual problems. Many generations of the same family live in one house and strong loyalties develop. Eventually, of course, someone must move, but wherever he goes he is liable to offend either his own family or that of his bride. By a wise tradition, the diviner must be called in when a new house is planned. The decision is referred to the heavenly powers and thus the new family finds its house site without anyone being offended. We can find lingering memories of such traditions even in Modern Europe. In Germany, once the main beam of the roof is in position, a bush is tied to it and a party is held to inaugurate the main stage of the building.

Opposite The mud built compound houses of the Nigerian town of Kano. *Below* A handsome four-poster bed in Knole House, Kent.

Today the ideal is the separate house for the small family unit of mother, father and children, but in earlier days and in other parts of the world, such a reduced household would have seemed a poorly restricted community. Grand-parents and grand-children lived with parents under the same roof and, except in the very poorest homes, there would be servants too, living in or coming in every day. The result was not only a large household but one in which people of all ages had a place. The old were looked to for advice and the young for entertainment and help with the household chores.

Ours is in fact obsessively 'private' age, and the history of the western house seems to reflect that search for privacy. Early in the middle ages, the great hall provided eating and sleeping and living accommodation for all but the family of the lord himself. Even their small retiring room adjoining the hall was only used at night. Gradually more and more private rooms were added. A solar for the ladies to retire to, a bower for the other members of the family, and so on. By the nineteenth century, a great mansion had separate rooms for almost every conceivable activity: breakfast room, dining room, morning room, living room, billiard room, smoking room, private boudoirs and, of course, special wings for guest rooms and servants' quarters. Although the house sheltered so many people, their privacy was so well guarded that if they should so wish they need hardly ever meet at all.

In the past, religion held a central place in people's lives and came naturally into their homes. The shrines of the household gods can still be seen in houses at Pompeii, and in ancient China and Japan the altar of the ancestors or the gods held an honoured place. In Russia, icons provided a focus of worship and, even today, in devout Catholic homes the world over, a candle can be seen burning before a holy picture with the figure of a patron saint nearby. Orthodox Jews may still follow the biblical injunction to place certain sacred texts on the doorpost of the house. For centuries, Protestant families began the day with prayers presided over by the head of the household and the family bible was one of the most treasured possessions. Today, religion has little obvious place in the home, apart from a vaguely religious picture in a bedroom, perhaps. It can be seen as the last vestige of the idea of veneration and awe that once was a central part of the human experience and as such found expression in the homes of men and women.

Top A shrine to the household gods in a house of ancient Herculaneum. *Above* This early nineteenth-century painting, *The Cotter's Saturday Night*, shows a humble family preparing for Sunday. The family bible took the place of the shrine of the household gods in many Protestant families from the Reformation to the nineteenth century.

The magnificent billiard room of Halton House
Buckinghamshire, England.

PHIL—
HERE'S A SIMPLE
IDEA YOU MIGHT
COPY FOR YOUR
BILLIARD
ROOM

The isolation of people from one another in self-contained dwellings is comparatively recent, even in Europe. In other cultures, the layout of the houses proclaims a sense of community. They are often grouped in compounds; cooking, washing, eating and conversation are public activities and the families only retire to their separate houses for sleep. The same kind of communal living arrangements were also to be found in China, where a number of houses might be grouped round a series of interconnecting courtyards. It is now returning to the West as architects react against the semi-detached world of garden cities and housing estates. Housing estates like the ones at Blackheath, designed by Eric Lyons, aim to bring back something of the atmosphere of a village community. Instead of individual gardens, the houses share a handsome landscaped park which spreads around them, while the placing of the units encourages families to share and mix. Designing like this for 'to-getherness' is increasingly common on both sides of the Atlantic, as if modern man, aware of his isolation from his neighbours, is looking to re-establish community links.

Even the squalid rows of back-to-backs of Victorian industrial city streets had a strong sense of community. The people who moved into them from the villages had been used to village life. People went freely in and out of one another's back doors and the chat over the garden fence was a real social activity. Despite the cruel hardships of industrial life, people met and gave one another strength to build something in the midst of the machine-dominated slum.

Unlike machines people are not well-ordered. They are untidy and passionate, their homes are homes of love and anger, worry and achievement and of unpredictable people both young and old. No machine has yet been devised that will really serve for living in. It can provide the facilities of hygiene and the comforts of warmth and convenience, but once life starts inside it, things are liable to be rearranged in ways that the designer may not have bargained for.

Even so, architects have generally tried to impose unity, as far as possible, on house interiors. Fontaine and Percier, Napoleon's architects, had this to say: 'Furniture is too closely connected with the decoration of the interior for the architect not to be involved in it. If the spirit of the house's decoration is divided from the building it will . . . make the essential forms disappear.' The interiors of Josef Hoffman's magnificent Palais Stoclet in Brussels certainly give the formal elegance of the exterior a new and opulent dimension. Less magnificent, but no less imaginative, was the house that the English architect, Charles Annesley Voysey, built for himself at Chorley Wood in 1900. Everything, even the keyholes and door hinges, is designed by him. The result of such schemes is indeed a magnificently consistent unity, but they are in danger of giving a static, museum-like quality to the living environment.

Despite the contrast between the cramped terraces of nineteenth century industrial towns (*opposite top*) and the comfortable landscape setting of Eric Lyons houses at Blackheath, London, (*opposite bottom*) both encouraged a friendly and communal life style. *Top* The Palais Stoclet, Brussels, designed in 1905 by Josef Hoffman is one of the last great European town mansions. *Above* The house that the architect C. A. Voysey built for himself at Chorley Wood, England in 1900.

17

Two superb miniature paintings done in the early fifteenth century by the Flemish Limbourg Brothers, as illustrations for a Book of Hours—a devotional handbook for the religious year. The prayers for each month begin with a picture and calendar for the month. Here we see (left) January and the day of gift giving. The Duke of Berri, for whom the book was done, sits before the fire on a bench covered in drapery. On the wall hangs a superb tapestry of a battle scene. Above February, a peasant family dries out after the day's work. Left below An illustration from another Calendar shows wine being drawn from kegs in a cellar.

In times of change people have often looked to their houses as symbols of security. From the late years of the eighteenth century, as the industrial revolution gathered momentum, designers began to revive styles of the past, as if to hold the machine age at bay. Later, architects like Norman Shaw and Philip Webb, were still drawing on the past to evolve a comfortable and relaxed pattern of living, consciously at odds with the mass-production technology of the nineteenth century. In the 1870s, William Morris and his friends founded 'The Firm'. It was to make by hand the furniture and furnishings for the 'Red House', designed for Morris by Philip Webb. It was a revolt against the machine age, but it was not very successful. By 1900, other skilled designers were working in the mass-produced market and house building has now come to rely heavily on factory made materials and fabrics undreamed of by Morris. Yet the popularity of artificial stone and other substitutes for natural materials, unpleasant as they are, shows how reluctant people are to make the final break with the habits of the pre-industrial centuries.

'Everyman's house should not only be to him a castle for security but a field for the display of individual taste and through it of individual character.' So wrote the craftsman William Watt, a contemporary of Morris's. The character of modern man, despite the relentless encouragement of *avantgarde* engineers and architects, is deeply conservative. His houses express the fact, as though he was determined they shall be homes and not machines for living in.

Top French art nouveau style room setting, 1902.
Centre The 'Red House', Bexleyheath, Kent.
Above Kelmscott Manor, Oxfordshire, England—the historic house that William Morris, pioneer of new relaxed styles of domestic designs, made his home. *Opposite* Throughout history, management of the landed estates has been important economically to great house owners.

Homes in a Landscape

In this chapter we look away from the house to its environment. For most of history, this has provided the house-builder with his materials and has set him problems of climate, often severe ones. Yet, from a very early stage, man has not been content merely to cower away from the natural world in the best shelter his ingenuity could devise. Like the beaver, damming rivers and demolishing young woodland to build its lodges, humankind has modified that environment – and on a massive scale. Its settlements have been surrounded by farms and its houses were set in gardens.

The earliest civilisations began to develop after the invention of agriculture in neolithic times and soon men were modifying the environment for pleasure as well as necessity. The Hanging Gardens of Babylon were one of the wonders of the ancient world and Roman villas were surrounded by gardens. Those at Laurentia were Pliny's pride and joy and wall paintings at Pompeii give us an idea of what a Roman garden looked like. Clipped hedges line sandy or gravelled walks, fountains play and behind them birds fly among the branches of ornamental trees and shrubberies. At exciting excavations in Fish-

bourne, England, archaeologists have even been able to uncover the bedding trenches, filled with green loamy soil and marled with lime, which were prepared by a Roman gardener close on two thousand years ago. As in the paintings at Pompeii, they flank wide paths, forming alcoves for statuary, fountains and single ornamental trees. The ceramic pipes, that once supplied the water for the fountains, still lie in their trenches just under the topsoil.

Before work could be begun on the large site at Fishbourne, it had to be levelled; the top soil was stripped and stored in piles and hundreds of tons of gravel were laid. After this preparation, the buildings of the villa began to rise round a large courtyard in which the formal garden was laid out. The main range of buildings was approached along the wide path flanked with fountains and statuary and its structure was camouflaged so as to give the impression of another garden beyond. The foundation wall was painted green, and white lattice fences, carefully trained flowering trees and a row of fountains completed the effect. On another side of the court, a dazzling white colonnade was partly masked by scores of rose trees.

Throughout the ages gardens and plants have been a natural part of houses whether in town or country. *Above* a courtyard in the House of the Vetii at Pompeii where a cloistered walk round the garden provides welcome shade from the hot Mediterranean sun. *Right* A merchant from some Netherlands town during the middle ages, walks in his garden and has a word with the chief gardener.

One of the piquant parallels which suddenly highlight the basic similarities between people no matter how different their cultures. *Above left* is *'The Swing'* by the eighteenth century French painter Fragonard (*above right*) a miniature from the Kangra school of Indian painting about 1800. *Left* Part of the beautiful gardens at Hidcote Manor, Gloucestershire.

Formal gardens like these have always been part of the European tradition. There were gardens for relaxation as well as for elegant display, even at Versailles the most formal of all Europe's palaces. In the grounds, remote from the palace with its geometric paths, flower-beds and pools, are hidden groves and glades where the casual young courtiers of an earlier age walked, made love and played garden games. The paintings of French artists like Watteau and Fragonard have caught the memory of this idyllic life for us. One of the most famous of all these scenes is Fragonard's *The Swing*. Pushed by the hand of an amorous gallant, the carefree young lady is thrilled and frightened at the same time like any girl on a fair-ground swing today – or even like her sister from an aristocratic family in India, who was painted at about the same time.

The two pictures make a delightful parallel to remind us that people the world over tend to enjoy themselves in much the same way, even though the assumptions and values of their cultures may be widely different. Such difference is found in the attitudes of East and West to the garden itself. In imperial China, the garden was a place of mystery and meditation on the place of man in nature. It was often designed to the personal specifications of the cultured house-holder. Doorways and windows were seen as frames for unexpected, dramatic or beautiful vistas. The garden was meant to be an extension of the house. It was a private landscape, but it embodied the eternal principles found in nature of which man was but a part.

In the West, where men see themselves as observers of nature rather than part of it, interest in landscape for its own sake came comparatively late. The medieval walled garden, with its formal flower beds and central fountain, was a secret place but, far from being a model of natural landscape, it was a retreat from the unruly and disordered reality of nature. The imagery was of an otherworldly paradise, an idyllic glimpse of heaven in the midst of a fallen world. After all, in the Biblical story, life began in the Garden of Eden where all was peace and fruitfulness.

With the Renaissance, Italy emerged as the natural leader in garden design. The theme was still formal but the inspiration was now from classical Rome. Statues of antiquity were set in the grounds and the geometrical approach we first saw at Fishbourne was reinterpreted. As the art moved north to France, it became still more abstract and rigid in its disciplining of nature.

The eighteenth century witnessed a revolution which started in England and led to the destruction of many formal gardens and their conversion into naturalistic landscapes. Men like 'Capability' Brown and William Kent made the garden into a park of wide views and rolling lawns. The gravel paths of the flower gardens round the house gave place to grass planted with a cloud of tumbling luxuriant blooms and clumps of shrubs.

It is interesting that one of the most dramatic of English gardens was planted by an American. In 1907, Hidcote Manor in Gloucestershire was bought by Lawrence Johnston. There was a stream in the valley and the trees included a fine clump of beech and a cedar of Lebanon. Apart from this the site, a windswept hillside of limestone soil, seemed unpromising. First the slope was terraced and then planted with hedges to act as windbreaks. They also linked a series of alcoves and these were planted with flowers from all over the world, set in carefully prepared bedding trenches. The little stream was lined with fine trees and shrubs. The simple acres had become a dream garden of exotic colours and scents – nature had been made to yield new delights.

In most civilisations, the rich have usually been able to make this kind of transformation scene. Often the very materials of the house were brought from far-flung districts. But, until quite recently, the builder of the average house was forced by transport costs and sheer technical problems to use the materials of the immediate countryside. As we shall see, traditional western building styles flourished in this context. The environment not only determined the materials used, often enough it also shaped the appearance of the building. In some parts of India, roofs are fitted with angled vanes which help to keep the interior cool by creating currents of air. The traditional shape of the Swiss chalet, wide and low, with gently sloping eaves, is ideally suited to a land of heavy winds and snowfall.

Different cultures have expected different things from their gardens. In medieval Europe the walled garden was a secret paradise of gentle dalliance; in the foreground, the lady with the key to the garden of pleasures leads a reluctant gallant.
The traditional wood-built chalet of Switzerland is a fine example of the adaptation of house building styles to their landscape.

Modern architects working in extreme climatic conditions make a close and technical study of them before beginning to design. In hot lands, trees and vegetation have more than a purely decorative function. Placed close to the house, they cool down the hot ground breezes and cut out the reflected heat that bounces off unshaded earth. To do this effectively, they must be planted close to the building, which gives the architect scope for imaginative effects. But the classical instance of a building adapted to environment has nothing to do with skills learned at architectural schools and colleges.

Opposite top Mud houses of Nigeria, painted and decorated with elaborate traditional designs. It seems that the type of tent used by the Nomads of Morocco (*below*), provided the model for the bamboo frame house being covered with its roofing of skins (*left*). The house is being built near Timbuctu in modern Mali and it is interesting to note that Timbuctu was the capital of a high Islamic culture in the middle ages, founded by Arabic nomads from the Sahara.

The Eskimo snow house, which makes survival possible in the most extreme climate on earth, is a dome of snow blocks about fifteen feet in diameter and nine or ten feet high. It is approached through a long snow tunnel cut about a foot lower than the floor level and with a right angle turn, while the sleeping quarters are on a raised snow platform round a central aisle—all precautions against draughts. Heat and light are supplied by a small blubber-burning lamp, which, with the body heat of the people, melts the snow so as to seal over the joints in the walls and roof with a thin film of ice. Skins are then slung across the 'ceiling' and a hole pierced in the roof to keep the ice from melting from the heat of the blubber lamp and form an insulating wall of air. Larger houses are equipped with a look-out window made of a pane of freshwater ice, more translucent than the salt-water variety and carefully transported from the summer campsite.

Few human structures so brilliantly exploit the available materials while simultaneously solving the problems of the environment as the igloo. It involves real constructional skill. The ideal material is firm snow from a drift formed by a single fall and thus free of the faults separating different strata of freezing. It is cut freehand into blocks with an ivory or bone knife. Next, the blocks are built up in a wide spiral leaning slightly inwards. The central block is placed in position from the inside. The process takes one hour.

In tropical zones like New Guinea, banana leaves or other natural fibrous substances are used for roof and walls over a frame of young saplings. The pyramids remind us of the greatness of ancient Egypt, but there is no trace of the houses of the people. Built of sun-hardened Nile mud, these have long since dissolved back into the soil. But mud is still used for house building in parts of Africa and dramatic designs can be achieved with it. In well forested regions, such as northern Europe, wood was the natural choice, while in districts of easily-quarried stone, that was used for all but the poorest dwellings.

Top left The spiral construction of the Eskimo snow house and the fresh water ice window can be clearly seen. *Above* Blocks are cut in a matter of minutes, freehand.

'From log cabin to White House' could indeed be a convenient short hand for a chapter in the history of house building. The typical home of the American pioneer, the log house, was a simple and sturdy shelter, demanding only a few tools and little expertise. After the trees had been felled and trimmed with an axe, an adze might be used to rough shape them and an auger was needed for drilling holes: doors and shutters were hung on wooden pegs or, in some cases, leather hinges. The walls were of logs, laid one above the other between retaining posts and the roof was of heavy planking. Daubed with mud, the house was moderately well weather-proofed, but the window openings, although sometimes covered with translucent waxed paper, inevitably made for draughts. The floor was usually of rammed earth, though 'puncheons', split logs with the flat side face up, might be used. Building a house was a communal effort and a good deal of fun must have been had by all since at a 'house raising' the future owner threw a party for his friends in return for their work.

Top left A riverside dwelling in Thailand.
Left The mud houses of the Dogon tribe in Mali are windowless to keep out the sun. *Above* In the Trobriand islands yams mean wealth and prestige and are stored in special houses.

Two aspects of town houses in Italy. *Right* The stately fourteenth century Venetian palace of the Ca d'Oro. *Below* A back street slum in Naples.

ALWAYS HANG OUT YOUR DUDS AT NIGHT
YOU WOULDN'T WANT YOUR NEIGHBORS TO SEE
THIS — WOULD YOU?

Left Medieval town housing. In the right foreground a woman is at work on a loom in the ground floor room of the house.
Below An old apartmenthouse in Kowloon, Hong Kong. In towns the world over, land was expensive and at a premium, housing necessarily tended to be somewhat cramped.

As the frontier of White America was gradually forced westward into the great plains, the log cabin gave place to the 'sod house'. This was built of three-foot sods of turf laid in courses like bricks. The walls were then smoothed with a spade and might be plastered with clay and ashes. The roof was thatched or covered with more sods. Even by the standards of the log cabin, the result was a dirty and insalubrious abode. The windows were necessarily small and after any heavy rains loose earth and mud seeped into the house and the roof had often to be replaced.

The log house had probably been introduced to America by settlers from Scandinavia and central Europe. In England, the basic type of wood construction was a frame structure, in its most primitive form the 'cruck' house. The roof tree was supported at either end by two inverted V's of timber, the 'crucks' and the walls were made on upright timber frames. The technique is ancient. Describing German houses, the Roman historian tells us that first the builders erected two forks and then wove bushes and branches between them, finishing the walls off with a covering of mud.

In the middle ages, the wood frame house was common in France, Germany and England in both town and country. After the frame had been put up the walls were clad with brush wood – the 'wattle' – and then covered with mud and plaster – the 'daub'. When brick became fashionable, it was used in the same way within the frame, but it was basically ill-adapted to this kind of fill-in work. Even so, the result could be extremely decorative and geometric effects could be achieved

that almost have the qualities of modern abstract paintings. Hundreds of fine examples of this kind of house can still be seen and many districts, such as the West Midlands of England and the Welsh Marches, derive their characteristic houses from the handsome black and white timber-frame buildings.

The result of traditional building methods was to make the house seem to belong to its landscape. Even a great house like Haddon Hall in Derbyshire, England, nestling in its wooded hollow, does not seem out of place. Modern materials and good transport, however, have meant that it is usually cheaper to use artificial materials and so modern housing rarely gives that sense of belonging. If the owner can afford it, the good architect will try to choose materials that harmonise and some outstanding results can be achieved, like the house at Cave Creek in the Arizona Desert, designed by Soleri and Mills. It is part excavated out of the hillside and part enclosed in masonry walls that harmonise perfectly. The roof is an incredible glass dome with sliding panels that open and shut automatically in response to temperature changes. Natural and artificial materials, sensitivity and technology have been combined to make a brilliant twentieth-century home.

This sixteenth century house at Clifford Chambers, Warwickshire, is a fine example of the half-timbered building style. The central block and the two gables remind us that in the middle ages the great hall with kitchens at one end and private rooms at the other was the basic big house design.

Below The square of Schwäbisch Hall in West Germany is dominated by a magnificent timber frame building. The central house has a wall painting of the kind which often decorated house fronts in the later middle ages. *Bottom* The magnificent stone pile of Haddon Hall, Derbyshire, England, has become almost part of its landscape.

Towns, Cities and Space

Human dwellings have very rarely stood alone in the natural environment. Men and women are sociable beings and they have always tended to live in groups. At first they seem to have been largely nomadic, but with the evolution of the arts of cultivation about 10,000 BC, societies began to live in more permanent settlements. The pattern of society inevitably began to change but the settlements also presented some practical problems of which the chief was probably that of sanitation. When the nomad leaves an encampment he also leaves behind his sewage and litter and the attendant dangers to health that beset the village or town dweller. As towns grew, these problems naturally mounted. The town house has to fulfil different functions from the country house and in this and the next chapter we shall look at some of these different functions. The first thing to notice about the town house is that its environment, the town, has been different at different times and in different places.

In modern terms the medieval town would seem little more than a glorified village. It was an environment in which urban and rural inter-penetrated and it continued like this for hundreds of years. Even in the main cities, a man could easily walk out into the surrounding fields. Names like Smithfield, half a mile from St Paul's Cathedral, hold a memory of the time when Londoners played football and other sports in the countryside only minutes from their homes. Over to the west stands the Church of St Martin-in-the-Fields, overlooking modern Trafalgar Square, while nearby Soho takes its name from the cries of the hunting field which once resounded over its thickets, groves, and fields.

As towns grew in size and the countryside became a little more remote, so the townsman took greater delight in his garden. Diaries and day-books lovingly record the purchase of plants for it, and dwell on the pleasure which the hard-headed merchant derived from a walk in his walled sanctuary where the cares of the world could for a time be forgotten. When Sir Thomas More wrote his *Utopia* in the early sixteenth century, he dreamed of a perfect city where every dwelling had a large garden 'inclosed round wyth the backe part of the streetes.' London was still small, but as the warren of streets grew the countryside retreated and the future pattern of urban life, cut off from the natural environment, was beginning to loom.

A new style of house would be needed. Medieval town houses opened straight onto the street and often stood in rows one house adjoining the other, but they were often wide farmhouses spreading easily along the street with room to spare. The true town house, which began to emerge in the fifteenth century, was built high rather than broad.

Houses like the magnificent eighteenth-century group on the Heerengracht at Amsterdam, have the main rooms on the first floor with steps leading up to the front door. The ground floor is given over to kitchen, store rooms and some servant quarters. In France and Germany, the main entrance was usually at ground level with a passage leading through to the staircase up to the main first floor. The kitchens and store rooms were on either side of the passage.

The Heerengracht in Amsterdam is one of Europe's finest streets and number 475, shown here, is one of that street's finest mansions. *Opposite top* An eighteenth century view of Amsterdam and (*opposite bottom*) the interior of a town house on the Spaarne, Haarlem, Netherlands.

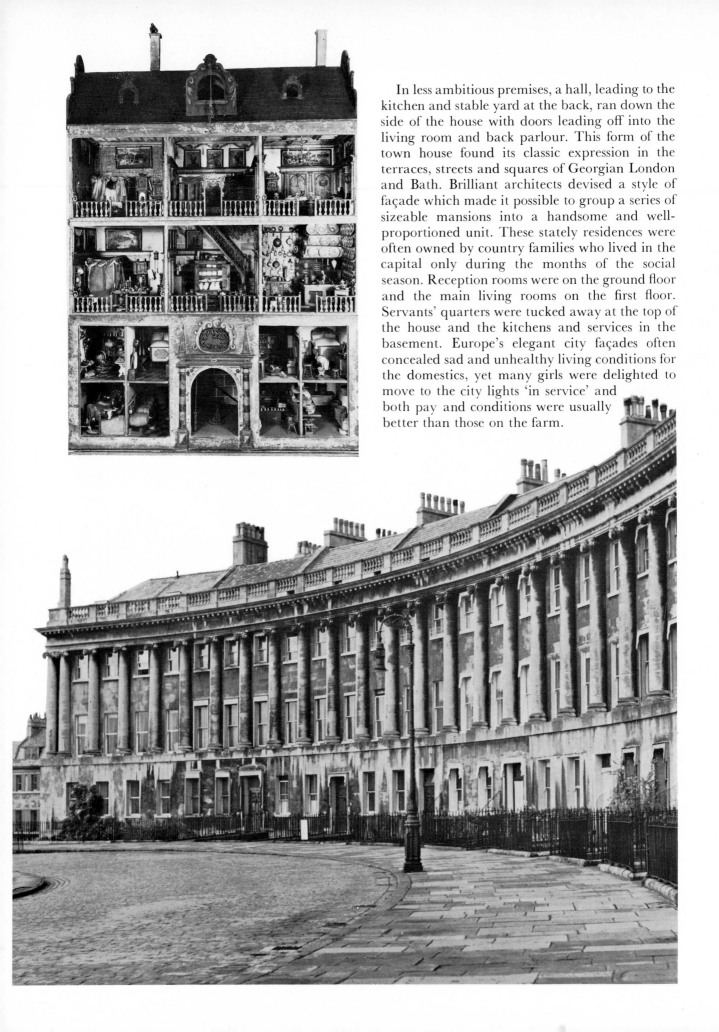

In less ambitious premises, a hall, leading to the kitchen and stable yard at the back, ran down the side of the house with doors leading off into the living room and back parlour. This form of the town house found its classic expression in the terraces, streets and squares of Georgian London and Bath. Brilliant architects devised a style of façade which made it possible to group a series of sizeable mansions into a handsome and well-proportioned unit. These stately residences were often owned by country families who lived in the capital only during the months of the social season. Reception rooms were on the ground floor and the main living rooms on the first floor. Servants' quarters were tucked away at the top of the house and the kitchens and services in the basement. Europe's elegant city façades often concealed sad and unhealthy living conditions for the domestics, yet many girls were delighted to move to the city lights 'in service' and both pay and conditions were usually better than those on the farm.

Dolls' houses, when they leave the nursery and go into the museum, are a useful record of earlier living styles. This is a magnificent seventeenth century example from Germany *(opposite)*. Either side of the street entrance are the storage, stables and kitchens and above them, on a mezzanine floor, the servants quarters. *Right* Even on this reduced scale the splendour and elegance of Cumberland Terrace, Regent's Park, is obvious. *Bottom left* In the eighteenth century the terrace became the classic style for the town house. The Royal Crescent, Bath, shows it at its glorious best; the cramped and ill proportioned nineteenth century 'housing' *(bottom right)* at its worst.

A new kind of townscape had been born. With narrow gardens and uniform frontages, it was uncomprisingly urban. Service roads at the back provided access to the mews where carriages and horses were housed. It is an ironic reflection on our age of progress that the coach-houses now shelter automobiles, for whose sake we are destroying so much of the elegance of the past, while the cramped quarters above them, once occupied by stable hands, are now smart apartments for the wealthy. The actual houses themselves are, of course, too expensive for any single family to live in. Some are divided into flats, most into offices or consulting rooms, others are hotels. Inevitably their magnificently proportioned interiors have been drained of the original atmosphere and sense of style.

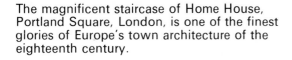

The magnificent staircase of Home House, Portland Square, London, is one of the finest glories of Europe's town architecture of the eighteenth century.

Above The cool refinement of the Etruscan Room in Home House, seems to sum up our notions of the aristocratic life-style of eighteenth century Europe. *Top* Hogarth, however, painted what he saw as the extravagance and debauchery behind London's elegant façades.

Left Another part of the Regent's Park Estate designed by John Nash in the early nineteenth century. The small window panes were a vital element in the proportions of this type of façade; comparison with Bath's Royal Crescent (page 36) as it is today shows how the modern passion for large windows can destroy the architect's intentions.
Below Apsley House, Hyde Park, London, was a fittingly grand mansion for national hero. It was the home of the Duke of Wellington during the first half of the nineteenth century.

Great cities have of course generally been congested places. They grew up around trading posts, or a castle, a palace or perhaps a famous temple. The houses clustered round the focus of activity, whatever it may have been. There was little room for the spacious villa in a Roman city. In place of low buildings round courtyards, all houses, except the palaces of the great, rose above a ground floor given over to shops, offices or public baths. Residential apartments were in the storeys above. A similar type of residential pattern developed in the towns of medieval Italy. There noblemen were involved in commerce from early times and had their main residences in the crowded towns. In contrast, the aristocracy north of the Alps lived apart, in their castles. An Italian nobleman who wanted that kind of security had to build high-rise in the urban manner and such lofty towers can still be seen at San Gimignano. More often however, the well-born merchant family simply lived on the first and second floors of a large house, renting out the ground floor to shopkeepers and craftsmen and the upper floors to poor students or professional men, like lawyers and doctors, who were very much social inferiors of the landlord.

Of course there was real opulence on the 'grand floor' or the *piano nobile*, where the aristocratic owner lived and, to keep the floors separate as far as possible, these great houses often had an outside staircase. This was as much for security as for reasons of snobbery. European cities of today are much safer places than they were even a century ago. Ground floor windows often had iron grilles, either cemented permanently into the stonework or secured by locks and chains over shop windows at night, when murderers and thieves prowled the ill-lit streets. On one notable occasion, King George II of England was even robbed in the garden of his palace at Kensington.

'Not far from Charing Cross dwelleth an honest young man, who being not long married and having more rooms in his house than himself occupieth . . . to make a reasonable commodity [profit] and to ease the house rent, which as the world goeth is none of the cheapest, letteth forth a chamber or two . . .' So begins a short story by Shakespeare's contemporary Robert Greene. It was the same the world over. Congestion may have made city life hazardous, but land values forced many people to let rooms, even when, as our 'honest young man' found out, to open your house to the public also might mean opening it to thieves.

A street in San Gimignano, Italy dominated by the towers of medieval aristocratic town houses.

Even in the status conscious society of Louis XIV's France, prosperous gentlemen rented out the ground floor of their town residences to traders and their families to help pay the building costs. In addition, of course, they might own other properties simply as investments. The architect J. F. Blondel advised that to distinguish it from these mere apartment houses the family residence should have a fine portico entrance. In fact, finding accommodation in seventeenth-century Paris could be arduous. A young travelling craftsman from Bavaria tells how he saw FURNISHED ROOMS TO LET in large red letters on several doors. At the first he had a narrow escape from an 'insolent' young landlady with a houseful of 'bold-mannered girls'; in another house he overturned a trash can in the dark hallway leading to the room, which turned out to house a crowd of chimney sweeps each sleeping on a pile of filthy straw. He did eventually find a top floor room in an agreeable house.

He was lucky; many a stranger in town found himself paying extortionate rent for poor rooms. Slum landlords are as old as towns. There was little control of rents in ancient Rome. But the city fathers did impose a height limit of seventy feet on apartment blocks in an attempt to stop unscrupulous owners who often built too high for safety or even added makeshift penthouses to the roofs of already overpopulated blocks. Jerry-built housing was as common in the city that produced the Colosseum as it is today, and as well as the lofty blocks, the balconies of ordinary houses, where families could be seen of an evening taking the air or eating supper above the street, were an additional hazard.

For the flat dweller, deprived of a garden, the balcony has always been a kind of outpost in the natural environment. It is at least as old as ancient Assyria and even then was causing problems for the authorities, though not necessarily of public safety. On the completion of a superb ceremonial way through the midst of his capital of Nineveh, King Sanherib (about 700 BC) was determined that it should not be encroached on by balconies from private houses. In an edict on the matter, he invoked sanctions of a kind not generally available to our modern planning authorities: quite simply, anyone building such a balcony could expect to be impaled on the finials of his own roof!

This was perhaps a little extreme, but regulations have always been necessary in cities. Land was so valuable in medieval cities that the upper storeys of the houses were built out over the street until they almost touched. Bye-laws in seventeenth-century Holland tried to control the degree of overhang and to establish a minimum height from the street. Contravention could result in the destruction of the house. Most houses were built of wood and the danger of fire always loomed. The great fire of London in 1666 which destroyed most of that great city was only the best remembered of many such conflagrations. The wooden houses were ready fuel but still worse was the fact that it took only a few sparks to set their thatched roofs alight. Without efficient pumps or fire engines the best way of fighting a fire was to starve it of fuel by pulling down the houses in its path. One can easily imagine the bitterness of people watching their homes being destroyed to save those of their neighbours. The houses of the new London were built with tiled roofs and some other towns, warned by London's example, made the use of tiles mandatory.

Since the middle ages, the traditional design of the European house has been outward-looking. Shop fronts giving directly on to the street, or the curtained windows of the main reception room also directly on the street have given the house in the town a public involvement. Even when the main apartments are lifted to first floor level they still look outward. But in many other cultures, the town house has presented blank walls to the street with the rooms grouped round an inner courtyard. The *atrium* or courtyard was the centre of the classic Roman suburban villa. In Kyoto, the earlier capital of Japan, the tourist can still see whole districts of old houses planned each around its courtyard garden. It is therefore very interesting to discover that this historic pattern of the inward-looking house has been revived by some modern European architects. This is reflected in a block of eight courtyard houses, sited on a busy thoroughfare in the heart of Chicago and designed by Y. C. Wong. A pupil of Mies van der Rohe, Wong had studied the master's designs for courtyard houses drawn up in the 1930s and it is because he decided to implement this age-old concept that his eight houses are in some ways more interesting than even the work of Rietveld and Le Corbusier. Surrounded by towering apartment houses and city streets, the houses present a bland exterior with a simple brick wall, pierced at rare intervals with doors. But within, each of the eight families enjoy a quiet retreat from the city. The rooms of the house look into one another through plate glass across the courtyard so that the community of each family need not be broken up. But each separate family is still rigorously divided from the others. In this way an ancient idea has been adapted to modern man's urge for privacy.

Gerrit Rietveld's Schröder House at Utrecht or Le Corbusier's renowned Villa Savoye near Paris are landmarks in twentieth-century domestic architecture. They are also, as would be expected from such masters, superbly planned for actual living. The Rietveld house is particularly interesting since in its provision for rooms to serve a variety of functions it anticipates a common feature of modern interior design. After centuries of accommodating each aspect of living with ever more specialist rooms, western man is being forced by the pressure of space in his cities to return to more 'open plan' living. Of course it is still a far cry from the all-purpose hall with which the history of the European house properly began, but an architect's plan designating a single room for 'kitchen-dining-living' in the house of 'a gentleman', would have been unthinkable in the nineteenth century.

Left Norman Shaw's Old Swan House in Chelsea, London, shows that the eclectic mixture of styles that became so popular in the nineteenth century could produce truly beautiful houses.

Top Le Corbusier's Villa Savoye, at Poissy, France, is a landmark in the history of modern house architecture. He said that the living area and its hanging garden should give views right to the horizon. The house was at home in its landscape. *Above* The Villa was built in 1931. Part of its revolutionary design was the fact that it had no façade, it was meant to open out on its environment in all four directions.

At the Big House

The household which Pliny described for us was a sizeable establishment. To him and his family it was a modest country place, with an estate big enough to provide a steady income but not cripplingly expensive to run. Buying a new estate was a matter for thought. Pliny, faced with the opportunity of acquiring the lands adjoining his own villa weighed things up carefully. One obvious advantage was that the two properties could be run by the same steward and share other staff and facilities, such as equipment. Secondly, the land was fertile and the additional vineyards and woods would increase the family income. But the times were bad, tenants were leaving the land for work elsewhere and the previous owner had managed the estate badly so that it would take some time to recover its natural fertility. Moreover, half the enjoyment of having a number of estates was to have them in different localities. A change of air was always pleasant and often good for the health, while just travelling from one of one's possessions to another was a pleasure.

There were villas like Pliny's, intended primarily for pleasure, throughout the empire, but there were many others, immensely bigger, intensively cultivated as capitalist agricultural investments. In fact, as the cities of the Roman empire began to decay, these estates became the centres of economic life. The French word for town, *ville*, is derived from the Latin word *villa*. In this chapter we take a look at the way in which the great country houses of Europe, from the time of the Romans onwards, were a major factor in the economy and social life of the locality.

These vast estates were, of course, run by slave labour. The slave was an indispensable part of ancient civilisation. If he worked in the mines, in construction work or in the notorious galleys, he could expect a life of merciless exploitation. He had no personal status at law. Even as late as in fifteenth-century Florence a bill of sale gave the purchaser total rights over a slave and 'none might gain say him.' The domestic slaves were not always much better off. Pliny, describing a new estate he thinks of buying, observes that the tenants will have to be given a fresh chance with new equipment and a better type of slave for, he says, 'I do not employ chained slaves.' But many landowners did. Such workers were kept in shackles when they were not actually working and were worked until they died. Buying new slaves was usually cheaper than the 'running costs' of keeping old ones alive. Employment in the house itself was no guarantee of humane treatment.

But there were slaves who might enjoy some prestige. Private tutors were often slaves in the technical sense, but they held complete control over the well-born children under their charge and their learning was often respected by their owners. Of course there were humane slave-owners like Pliny. He held the unconventional view that the household 'provides the slave with a country and a sort of citizenship'. He even allowed his slaves, who legally had no property, to make wills and bequeath their few personal effects to other members of the household. He also saw that they had good medical care. As a result he suffered from the 'servant problem', apparently the bane of householders since the beginning of history. Where other masters simply flogged, killed or sold off their slaves, Pliny wryly accepted the fact that people can be uncooperative. In one letter, we find him urging a friend to accept an invitation to stay at the villa, not only because he would enjoy himself but also because his arrival would wake up the staff: 'slaves lose all fear of a considerate master once they are used to him, but they bestir themselves at the sight of new faces.'

Centuries later, Petrarch described the slaves of his native Florence as the 'domestic enemy'. They too had no legal standing, but in the congested conditions of a medieval town house it was difficult to maintain a distance between master or mistress and slave. In fact, many mistresses were frankly frightened of the Central Asian slave girls brought back by the merchants from the markets of the Black Sea ports. They were tough and independent and soon learnt how to exploit a mistress with too much conscience to be ruthless and too little personal authority to command respect. Worse still, the girls were often unreasonably pretty, many a dusky beauty in the crowd scenes of the Italian painters of the period testify to that. The city law imposed a fine of a thousand florins on a man who seduced another's slave, but there was no law against what he might do with his own.

Top left Pliny's handsome villa was the centre of a large estate which provided the owner with a solid income. For his guests the delights of the seaside house counted more than the profitable acreage. *Left* The covered hall or *atrium* was the central part of a large Roman villa. Here we see one in a house of ancient Herculaneum, southern Italy.

Below A banquet in a medieval castle, King
John of Portugal entertains the English duke,
John of Gaunt. *Bottom* Food being taken from
the kitchen to a great man's table.

Right up to the nineteenth century, the great
houses of Europe were home for an army of
servants and household officers. They were also a
source of employment for scores of local people.
In the middle ages, even a minor baron kept as
many as thirty full-time men on the staff – a large
household needed many more. The organisation
was headed by the lord and his council of knights
and the day-to-day management of affairs was
in the hands of a household steward and an estate
steward. 'Day-to-day' it certainly was, for the
household steward was expected 'to account every
night . . . with the buyer, marshal, cook and other
officials. It is his duty also to take a tally of the
meat and fish which shall be cut up into portions
in his presence and counted as they are delivered
to the cook. It is his business to know precisely
how many farthing loaves can be made from a
quarter of wheat.' He was assisted by the 'ward-
rober' or accountant. Under them came: the
chaplain who also headed the clerical staff;
pantrymen in charge of the bread; butlers for
the wine; a baker; a brewer; a marshal who was
in charge of the horses; a blacksmith and others.

The household steward was usually a man of humble birth for whom the job itself was the fulfilment of an ambition. He might have begun his career with a short period of formal training. Since the thirteenth century, there had been teachers living at Oxford who offered courses in estate and household management. The senior of the two stewards, the estate steward, was usually a young nobleman who tended to look on his job as the beginning of a career aimed eventually at royal service. His job was to ensure the profitable running of far-flung lands. It could involve a good deal of travel round the country and carried heavy responsibilities. Since tenants usually paid their rents in kind rather than money, a great lord reckoned to move from one manor at regular intervals, as much to consume his rents as to supervise his property. Such moves involved additional work for the household, which might even include a full-time staff of carters, though more usually these were hired as required. Sometimes the baggage might include glass windows which were still a luxury and were taken by their proud owners from one house to another.

Top An estate steward supervising workmen in a great garden. *Above* A red-nosed household steward enthusiastically 'tests' the wine while his masters carouse upstairs.

Since great houses are the homes of rich men
it is not surprising that they have always been
filled with luxuries and signs of wealth. In ancient
Rome, Cicero declaimed against the newly-
imported carpets from Persia which, he claimed,
were making people soft and undermining the
austere virtues of the Republic. The high living
that marked the Rome of the Caesars which
followed is perhaps best symbolised by the
notorious banquets that sometimes lasted for days
on end. Feasting was a big feature of medieval
life too. Not only did it show a man's wealth, it
also showed his generosity, thought to be an
essential quality of the great man. When the
fifteenth-century Earl of Warwick sat down to
dine, his servants and the beggars round the
palace were permitted as much of the roast meat
as they could carry away on their daggers or
knives. The art of feasting did not die out in the
Renaissance but new ways of disposing of excess
wealth were found. Duke Albrecht V of Bavaria
listed 1407 items in his collections of works of
art and curiosities and the collecting craze has
been growing ever since. Before the development
of the modern money market, jewellery and works
of art were a favourite means of investment and
for the aristocrat his mansion was not only his
home but also his treasure house.

The rich man in his castle,
The poor man at the gate,
God made them high and lowly
And ordered their estate.

This famous verse from the Victorian children's
hymn, 'All things Bright and Beautiful', summed
up an attitude that had governed human society
for thousands of years. Contrasts of wealth and
poverty were accepted, notably by the rich, as
part of the eternal scheme and even the poor, for
whom life could be hard and cruel, found some
comfort in the thought they, too, had a place in
the hierarchy of society presided over by God. At
its best, the attitude of rich to poor was one of
paternalistic concern; that of the poor tenantry
to 'the folk up at the big house', was one of
deference. When the lord and his family treated
their people with humanity and understanding
this deference might be founded on respect, even
affection. But the cottager always knew that he
could easily be evicted from his house, so that the
most basic considerations forced him to accept
his lot.

Even among the underprivileged, social status
was something to be prized. The gentry treated
their servants with a patronizing interest. The

Top left Cleaning the copper was one of the
worst chores in a great kitchen yet the
charming *Scullery Maid* painted by J. B. Chardin
seems resigned to her lot. *Above* The Kitchen of
Queen Victoria's Swiss Chalet, built for the royal
children. *Top right* A house party playing
croquet at Alton, Hampshire, 1865. *Right* The
kitchen staff of Keele Hall pose for their
photographs in the 1890s.

48

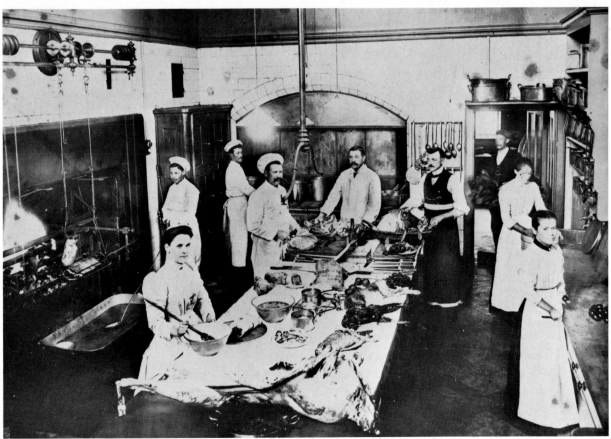

49

servants, for their part, felt distinctly superior to the craftsmen and labourers 'at the gate.' Their pay was generally better and their position much more secure. In years of bad harvest the ordinary people had to tighten their belts, a craftsman might even have to sell his tools – his only capital investment – to live, but the rich were the last to suffer and their servants shared to a lesser extent in their privilege.

The structure of class consciousness held good even in the servants' hall. The butler of a nineteenth-century establishment had his own suite of rooms and even his own servants; the lower orders had to show him respect. A scullery maid who presumed to speak to the head housekeeper without permission could expect to be punished or even sacked.

The modern visitor to the great houses of the past can easily forget the considerable economic investment they represented. It has been estimated that even in the middle ages, when money was less important in the economy than it is today, a third of the cost of building went in wages and surviving accounts show clearly that the overall cost of a great mansion might run into millions of our present currency. In those days, the most important buildings were castles and cathedrals

The owner of Ballingdon Hall, Sudbury, Suffolk, decided to 'move house' when new buildings threatened to spoil his view. In the good old days the lord of a great house destroyed whole villages if they spoiled the vista.

and their designers were important men who could rise from the humblest beginnings to high positions in church or state. In the towns, wealthy merchants were building handsome halls for their guilds and fine mansions for their private use.

The building techniques used remained much the same up to quite recent times. Technical resources were limited, the pulley and winch were about the only types of machinery used, and horses and men provided the motive power. Rickety wooden scaffolding was sometimes used, or the working platforms were supported on poles let into holes in the completed sections of the wall. Much of the skilled work was done by travelling groups of stone-masons who developed a close brotherhood, like the guilds of merchants in the cities, on which the modern society of Freemasonry was modelled. The unskilled labour,

on the other hand, was recruited locally and so, from the moment it began to rise, the 'big house' brought money to its neighbourhood. As more and more families could afford to build great houses, the skills of the architect and stone-mason came into ever greater demand and increasingly masons found that they could get enough work in one area to make it worth settling down and developing a local practice.

Opposite left Building a castle. *Opposite right* A medieval artist's impression of the building of the Tower of Babel. Both pictures give a comprehensive survey of medieval building methods. Apart from the winch they were probably not very different from those used in the ancient world when the tower of Babel was in fact built.

51

The kind of profitable turmoil that the building of a great house could bring to its district is to be found in the case of Blenheim palace, at Woodstock in Oxfordshire, England. More than twenty quarries were used to supply the stone to the masons at work on the site. Cut from the living rock and then rough-shaped at the quarry, it had to be hauled several miles along simple earth tracks, which turned into quagmires after heavy rain. Sir John Vanbrugh, the architect, had specified an especially rare type of stone for the main steps and for years the palace was without a fitting entrance because of the cost and technical problems involved. At another stage, the building operations were held up because the wagoners demanded extra pay. Even in the early eighteenth century, money could speak still more powerfully than nobility. When Sarah, Duchess of Marlborough, (the client) refused to concede the pay rise, the carters simply quitted the job. Huge blocks of moss-covered stones can still be seen in the woods around the palace where they were left by a disgruntled labour force. But the job had already paid them well enough.

A big house might bring prosperity to an area, but it could also bring disaster. Its spreading parklands and elaborate, decorative gardens, demanded hundreds of acres and on many occasions the nobleman's pleasure grounds were provided at the expense of other people's homes and land. Probably the best-known example of the destruction of a community in the interests of a luxury palace is the village of Trianon, swept away at Versailles to provide the site for yet another mansion for the apparently insatiable Louis XIV. But there were similar cases all over Europe.

At Claydon in Buckinghamshire, England, the graveyard of the village church was moved to make room for the new grounds planned by the second earl Verney. The villagers protested against the desecration and forecast disaster for the family. In fact, the earl bankrupted himself in the extensions to the house and had to flee England to avoid his creditors. According to one tradition, he was found years later wandering around the deserted rooms, a broken old man, and was given shelter by one of his former servants. Many an old villager must have nodded in grim satisfaction at the fulfilment of the prophecy. The Dukes of Devonshire seem to have been spared such retribution, yet twice they adjusted the landscape round their place at Chatsworth in Derbyshire. During the eighteenth century, the farm buildings visible from the house were destroyed to improve its vistas and in the nine-teenth century the village of Edensor was demolished and rebuilt out of sight of the mansion.

Below Chatsworth House, Derbyshire, England, home of the dukes of Devonshire. *Right* The painted hall at Chatsworth. It is not surprising that the doings at such palatial mansions were the continual talk of their neighbourhoods.

FIX UP YOUR HALL LIKE THIS — IN YOUR SPARE
PAINTING TIME — AND YOU CAN IMAGINE YOU ARE
BACK IN THE SISTINE CHAPEL —

THEN YOU AND I WILL BE THE TALK OF YOUR
NEIGHBORHOOD

53

Once completed, such mighty palaces naturally became the focus of local society. Contemporary pictures show the forecourts and gardens swarming with elegantly dressed figures, some doubtless house guests but many of them curious tourists. A great house was always thronging with petitioners seeking favours from the great man or with retinues of visiting gentlemen, but members of the lesser gentry in the surrounding district took every opportunity to visit the place and be seen there. One can sense from the novels of Jane Austen, the fascination that surrounded everything to do with the big house and the central place it occupied in its locality. An invitation to visit was something to be treasured and proudly displayed to one's friends and one's rivals. A ball for the 'coming out' of the daughter or the coming-of-age of the son involved weeks of preparation for all those fortunate enough to be invited. Tailors and dress makers enjoyed a sudden upsurge in business while the preparations for the banquet might put good trade the way of the local provision merchants.

The owners of these big houses had no doubts about their own importance. The walls of their galleries were lined with family portraits – coats of arms were carved over doors and armorial beasts in stone were proudly mounted on the roofs – the house was approached through massive wrought-iron gates, guarded by lodges which were often sizeable houses in their own right, and from them up impressive tree-lined avenues. The art galleries of the world display paintings from the last five centuries of European houses and the scenes of luxury which were commonplace in their heyday, while the modern antique business builds its multi-million turnover on the superb hand-made furniture, porcelain ware and ornaments, gold and silver plate and cutlery that were

the essential equipment of a house of any size. The finest were made by craftsmen who brought a life of artistic sensitivity and skill to their work. The names of the most famous are now revived in auctioneers' catalogues to the delight of collectors and the inflation of prices, but thousands of magnificent pieces come from long-forgotten masters. Local craftsmen in town and country provided a fund of expertise for the rich connoisseur even in the provinces.

The work was often in precious materials and the labour and skill of men were highly prized, so that although the modern flight from money has given the furniture and fittings of the past an inflated value, these things were never cheap. When a house was demolished, its fine fireplaces and panelling might be carefully removed either for sale or to be built into the new mansion, while the furniture and other equipment was carefully preserved and handed down from one generation to another. Especially prized pieces were bequeathed by men in their wills and Shakespeare's bequest: 'to my wife, my second best bed', although apparently something of a wry joke, was not unusual in any other respect.

We pride ourselves, perhaps, on the rapidity of change in our society and this change is often reflected by the speed with which we change our homes and the objects in them, but in earlier days things were built to last. To be surrounded with objects that had served one's family for generations as many people did, gave life a quality of security and continuity that today seems to have been lost for good.

Left The home of the Brontë family, at Haworth, Yorkshire, was typical of many an English vicarage. *Right* The cottage at Blaise, Gloucestershire, was to the romantic ideal of the nineteenth century, a perfect model of solid homeliness and rustic simplicity. *Top right* This nineteenth-century painting is called *Too Early*. A smart musical evening has been planned, but some of the guests have broken social convention by arriving too early. The lady of the house is giving the musicians their last instructions and two of the maids peep round the door to the servants' quarters before getting ready to serve the guests.

Homes fit for Gentlemen

In the first four chapters of this book the aim has been to discover something of the nature of the house and the place that houses, both large and small, have played in human history. At this point the perspective changes slightly to give the opportunity for more detailed descriptions of selected great houses in the Old World. We begin with some of the 'stately homes' of England.

During the middle ages, the English gentry tended to build their homes for strength and security. As late as 1540, Sir Richard Edgecumbe provided his new house at Cotehele, in remote Cornwall, with a sturdy gatehouse. By this time, the gatehouse was more generally an opportunity for display and ostentation, but Sir Richard had already been driven from his Cotehele estate once by the armed retainers of a neighbour and he did not intend that it should happen again. The great hall, with roof open to the rafters, is another reminder of the medieval past which gave Cotehele a somewhat old-fashioned air.

Left The main façade of Longleat, Wiltshire, home of the Marquis of Bath. *Below* The West Front of Woburn Abbey, Bedfordshire, home of the Duke of Bedford. *Bottom* The sturdy gatehouse of Cotehele House, Cornwall, clearly built to repel attackers.

The Tudor age was a great period of house-building. Henry VII had battled his way to the throne in 1485. His court was full of new families looking, like the new king, to establish their fortune. Then, in the 1530s, Henry VIII dissolved the monasteries. The vast wealth plundered from the Church, when it did not go to feed the extravagant policies of the king, poured into the pockets of new aristocracy. As its members competed in the building of magnificent houses, labourers found work in plenty and an army of skilled stone-masons was released. As a result the new houses often showed similarities of style to church buildings. At Leez Priory and Woburn Abbey, for example, the great house closely followed the ground plan of the monastery which it replaced, while at Longleat, the geometric tracery in the windows and the vast areas of glass are natural continuations in the late medieval Perpendicular style in English church building.

57

Lacock Abbey in Wiltshire went to Sir William Sharington. Like his friend Sir John Thynne of Longleat, he was one of the pioneers of the Italianate Renaissance style in England. He retained the medieval cloister, but remodelled it to achieve a surprisingly classical air, which is not obscured by later additions like the battlemented oriel windows which reflect the eighteenth-century taste for Gothic decoration. The house went by marriage to the Talbot family and it was here, in the nineteenth century, that William Henry Fox Talbot made his revolutionary invention of the positive-negative process which made popular photography possible.

Knole House in Kent passed into aristocratic ownership under Henry VIII. Externally it still looks much as it did when it was built in the 1450s for Thomas Bourchier, Archbishop of Canterbury, but in the early seventeenth century the interior was transformed for Thomas Sackville, first earl of Dorset, who had received the house from Queen Elizabeth. The rooms and galleries are still comparatively small, betraying their medieval origins, but the work for Sackville, in the reign of James I, together with an art collection amassed over generations, make Knole one of the most staggering show pieces among the stately homes of England.

Lacock Abbey, Wiltshire, was remodelled by its Tudor owner to give a fine blend of Gothic traditionalism and fashionable Renaissance Italian styles. Lacock was the home of Henry Fox Talbot who invented the photographic negative. This picture shows two of his friends taking tea outside the cloisters there.

58

Below The superb but rambling medieval pile of Knole House, Kent, like many a medieval great house, looks almost like a township. The room known as the 'King's Bedroom' at Knole with seventeenth century tapestries and furnishings.

The Russels were another family to rise to the nobility in the early Tudor age. The great house at Woburn stands on the site of yet another abbey given by the crown to a faithful supporter. In the early seventeenth century, the old Abbey buildings began to be replaced. The grotto room, no doubt inspired by Italian models, dates from this period. In the middle of the eighteenth century, the family, now dukes of Bedford, launched a rebuilding programme under the architects John Sanderson, Henry Flitcroft and Henry Holland. This period also left a fashionable fancy in the shape of the delightful Chinese dairy.

The magnificence of the Georgian exterior, set in the stately park-land designed by Humphrey Repton, is overmatched by the countless art treasures within, but a modern ducal public relations exercise has firmly established Woburn in the public mind as the home of one of England's largest wild game parks.

Europe's aristocratic families were, by and large, founded not by engaging gentry with chivalrous ideals, but by men with a shrewd eye for the main chance and a strong interest in money. When stupidity or extravagance made the going harder funds could easily be consolidated by marrying the daughter of a successful merchant; in whose veins the blood of competitive self-interest still flowed strong. Today, when taxation and death duties are seen as the enemies, the English aristocracy has shown itself worthy of its ancestors and has found ways of maing.its country estates at least pay for themselves.

For a family like the Russells, who can name a prime minister and the world-famous philosopher Bertrand Russell among its illustrious members, the intellectual problems of business management need present few problems. Moreover, at a time when tourism is a growth industry, the owner of an historic pleasure palace has much in his favour. In its age-long history the house has been many things. A shelter, a setting for display, a focus for family life and ancestral piety, or even a 'machine for living in'. Today, the stately home at least, has revealed another function – the house can be a profitable business enterprise.

Competition at the top of the stately home 'league' is brisk. One great Georgian house in the centre of England can be hired for business conferences, a little further north an enterprising owner even plays the organ to entertain his guests, while at least one palace runs a profitable garden centre in its grounds. But the glamour of a wild game park cannot easily be outdone and now one can hire professional game park consultants.

Over on the other side of England from Woburn, the Marquess of Bath, with the sales slogan of 'lions at Longleat', contests the honours for England's top game park. Yet Longleat, too, was once the site of a religious house, though St Radegund's Priory has long since disappeared. The great house was designed by Sir John Thynne, whose friends numbered Sir William Sharington of Lacock and Lord Burghley, Queen Elizabeth's great minister. It is likely that the architect Robert Smythson advised on the design and the

work, begun in 1540, took some forty years to complete. The first of the great Elizabethan houses, Longleat is also the most classical and it has features that were to be taken up and developed at Hardwick Hall, Burghley House and elsewhere. Its great height, the vast expanse of glass and the three-storeyed bays, thirteen in all, which jut out from the three façades, are all examples.

'God send us both long to enjoy her, for whom we have both exceeded our purses in these.' So wrote William Cecil, Lord Burghley, to Sir Christopher Hatton, another of Queen Elizabeth's ministers. He was speaking of the Queen and the houses that they, like many other courtiers, had built in her honour. Ennobled by a grateful sovereign in 1570, he had been in state service since the reign of Edward VI and was appointed chief minister to Elizabeth at her accession. He died in 1598 at the age of seventy-eight, still at the head of affairs. One of the greatest figures in English history, his steady and cautious wisdom was the ideal foil to the secretive, changeable, brilliant and autocratic queen. Together they kept England safe and prosperous during the half century when Europe was rent by religious and dynastic wars.

Opposite A painting of Longleat House in the days of its glory. *Above* The great saloon at Longleat.

The great court,
Burghley House,
Northamptonshire.

Burghley was also one of the gentleman-architects so common at that time – men who were anxious that their grand new homes should present to the world the appearance they thought accorded best with their own greatness. His interest in architecture is indicated in his letters, and French and Flemish influences can both be seen at Burghley House. Work began on the site, a manor house he had inherited from his father as early as 1553, but the place was not completed until 1587. For twelve years, in fact, he was absorbed with the building of his other great house at Theobalds in Hertfordshire.

The east range of Burghley containing the Great Hall with its superb double hammer beam roof, was the first to be completed. At the end of the seventeenth century, extensive redecorations were commissioned by the fifth earl of Exeter on his return from a tour of Italy. The Italian artist Verrio lived at the house for ten years and his 'Heaven Room' is a masterpiece of illusionistic painting. The earl's vast plans were not completed for a century, but during the eighteenth century the gardens were re-designed by Capability Brown in the naturalistic style he had made fashionable. As a result, Burghley House is a place of dramatic contrasts. Surrounded by its landscaped park from the age of elegance stands an uncompromising Elizabethan mansion, but within the scene changes again to surround the visitor with paintings of baroque flamboyance. The largest example of Tudor domestic architecture it is a monument to the varied talents of its statesman-architect.

The most completely authentic of all the Elizabethan mansions, perfectly preserved in structure, gardens and interiors, is Hardwick Hall in Derbyshire. 'In this glorious house,' the art historian Olive Cook has written, 'all the high aesthetic and intellectual excitement, the freshness, the intensity of expression, the swagger and vitality of the age find expression.' Its fine state of preservation is due to the fact that the Cavendish family, who inherited it, preferred their mansion at Chatsworth, so that Hardwick was spared the improvements of later generations. Even the gardens are virtually unaltered so that the Hall is approached along an undulating tree-lined road which holds back the glittering façade of glass and reflected sunlight till the last dazzling moment. The house faces south and so catches all the sun there is. 'Hardwick Hall more glass than wall,' ran the old saying. The building is the culmination of the Perpendicular tradition in domestic architecture. As at Longleat, Robert Smythson worked on the design, but the owner controlled it. Her coroneted initials, E.S., for *Elizabeth* (Countess of) *Shrewsbury*, look down from the dancing scrolls on the parapet. The job must surely have been the most harassing that Smythson ever accepted, for Bess of Hardwick, the richest woman in the land after the queen, was perhaps the most startling lady ever to have crossed the stage of English history.

The daughter of a humble squire at Hardwick, Derbyshire, she died with a personal income estimated in modern terms at six million pounds per annum before tax – three centuries before tax, to be precise. It came from four husbands, each of whom were persuaded, bewitched said some, to leave Bess their entire fortune. The first died, conveniently enough, only a year after his marriage to the fourteen-year-old Bess. The second, whom she wed 'at two of the clock after midnight', she seems to have loved. Certainly she only had children by him. But he had to sell up his estates in southern England and buy lands in Derbyshire from some of Bess's own relations so that his wife could remain close to her family. Her influence over her third husband brought furious complaints from his family. After his death and well-drafted will, Bess, now fifty, was still beautiful enough to seduce the earl of Shrewsbury, one of England's most eligible bachelors into marriage, but only after he had made large advance settlements on herself and her family. The marriage gradually broke up and in 1587 Bess left her husband to begin an ambitious rebuilding of her family manor at Hardwick.

Below The grand façade of Hardwick Hall surmounted by the builder's monogram, E.S. *Bottom* The Great Hall at Hardwick.

Three years later her husband died and he, too, left everything to her. Now, at the age of seventy-two, Bess embarked on her greatest work. She had already built four other mansions, among them the first house at Chatsworth, but Hardwick outshone them all.

Through the middle of the house rises a great stone staircase without balustrade or adornment. It gives an air of mystery to the place, slowly opening up unexpected vistas. Like every Elizabethan house, Hardwick has its Long Gallery, but none is so heavy with the atmosphere of a bygone age. The portraits that stare down on the modern tourist are presided over by pictures of Queen Elizabeth and Bess herself. With a characteristic overplus of luxury, these fine paintings hang against and partly obscure a set of magnificent Brussels tapestries. These were bought by Bess from Sir Christopher Hatton. She had the arms of the Hatton family covered by her own and the does, the Hatton badge, have been embellished with antlers and so converted into the stags of the Shrewsburys.

Top The staircase at Hardwick winding up through the middle of the house, is one of the great features of the place. *Above* The Great House from the south.

An unfriendly observer described Bess as a 'builder, a buyer and seller of estates, a money lender, a farmer, a merchant of lead, coals and timber.' She would have been unscathed. Centuries before the advent of women's lib she left a mark on the English scene that few men have equalled. Up to her death at the incredible age of ninety, she held her entourage in awe. It is said that she built so much and so consistently because of a prophecy that she would not die while she was building. She did die on February 13th, 'in a hard frost while her builders could not work.'

In 1550 Bess and her second husband William Cavendish began the building of a high, quadrangular, turretted house at Chatsworth. Mary Queen of Scots was held here for a time with the Earl of Shrewsbury, much to Bess's annoyance, her gaoler. Mary's room is still preserved at Chatsworth but the present house dates from much later. Reconstructions begun on the south front by William Talman in 1687 were completed from 1800 to 1839 by Jeffrey Wyatt. The handsome west front was apparently erected under the

Top Built during Elizabeth's reign, Chatsworth was extensively altered during the seventeenth and eighteenth centuries. The west front was built under the direction of the first Duke of Devonshire himself about 1705. *Above* Another view of the west front.

BETTE! I never knew you had to B---- + i... your Best shame on you!

The heavy and opulent furnishings of the Victorian age are handsomely represented by the pictures on this page. *Left* The library at Oxburgh Hall. *Below* The reconstruction of a Victorian parlour in the York Museum. The piano was indispensable for a family with any social standing; the parlour was the chief room in the house holding the family treasures.

Opposite page William Morris believed that the middle ages was a period when art was a living part of society and the craftsman had a life much more worthwhile than the nineteenth century industrial worker. This painting of *La Belle Iseult* by him is a reconstruction of a medieval interior and shows the kind of fabric designs that he reproduced on his wallpapers and curtains.

directions of the first duke of Devonshire. In the grounds, redesigned by Capability Brown, stands the Cascade House, from which a thrilling waterfall flows down a long stairway into the garden.

The palatial state rooms, as at Hardwick on the top floor, present a rich display of English domestic decoration. The wood carving, which would not have disgraced the renowned Grinling Gibbons, is in fact by Samuel Watson, an undeservedly neglected local genius. There are ceilings painted by Sir James Thornhill, the Italian painter Verrio and the Frenchman Laguerre, and also fine tapestries and furnishings from the early eighteenth century.

In the nineteenth century, the popular reputation of Chatsworth was based on the immense glass houses built for the sixth duke by his gardener Joseph Paxton. Using similar principles of construction, Paxton was the designer of the vast Crystal Palace which housed the Great Exhibition of 1851. The notion of the iron and glass construction, a remarkable anticipation of twentieth-century building methods, caught the imagination of the technology-minded Victorians so that every suburban villa with pretensions soon boasted a conservatory.

The Tudor boom in house building threw up houses of all kinds among them serviceable cottages for the growing class of yeoman farmers. The house of John Hathaway, at Shottery just outside Stratford-upon-Avon, is a handsome example. Its half-timbered structure, dating from the fifteenth century, is in a style known throughout Europe. Because Anne Hathaway was John's daughter and because the young William Shakespeare must many a time have walked her back there after a tumble in the hay, it has become one of the most famous houses in the world.

Between the cottage and the mansion came the manor house, such as the one begun by Lawrence Washington in the 1540s. The ancestry of George Washington can be traced back to County Durham in the late twelfth century. In the 1530s, Lawrence Washington moved south to Northampton, becoming mayor of the town and buying the manor at nearby Sulgrave. His house there remained in the family for a century after its completion, until 1659. Three years earlier, John Washington had emigrated to America. George was his great-grandson.

For two and a half centuries Sulgrave had the history of a typical English manor house. Successive owners changed the place, demolishing here and adding there but we can still see the porch,

Anne Hathaway's Cottage with the interior of the kitchen and the staircase.

Great Hall, great bed chamber and two adjoining rooms of the original house. In 1914, to celebrate a hundred years of peace between England and the United States, the house was bought by public subscription in England for presentation to the peoples of the two countries. A subsequent Anglo-American subscription made possible the restoration and furnishing of the house and a handsome endowment by the National Society of the Colonial Dames of America has made it possible for the Sulgrave Manor Board to maintain the structure and keep it open to the public in perpetuity.

In the right hand corner of the arch over the south porch there is a carving of the Washington family coat of arms. It is a silver shield crossed by two red bars below three red stars and it is plausible that this had some part in the origin of the 'Stars and Stripes'. Artistically the most important piece of furniture is the Hepplewhite chair now in the Chintz Bedroom which came from the Washington family home of Mount Vernon and once belonged to him. There are other outstanding pieces of English furniture from the sixteenth, seventeenth and eighteenth centuries, acquired at various times, but the great kitchen, probably the most popular room in the house, is unique since it was bought complete and represents an eighteenth-century kitchen with all its contemporary fixtures and equipment.

69

Sulgrave Manor, one of the very few homes in England that flies the flag of the United States, is a place of pilgrimage for many Americans. It is also a fine museum of life in a typical English house during America's colonial period, the kind of homestead that many of the original settlers remembered and tried to recreate in their new life across the ocean.

Below Sir Richard Edgecumbe's fine and sturdy house at Cotehele in Cornwall, a reminder that houses were still built as a means of protection for their owners. *Right and far right* Sulgrave Manor, Northants., with the American flag flying outside to commemorate the fact that this was the home of the Washington family for many years.

Above The hall in the Washington family home at Sulgrave Manor.

We find an American connection of a different kind at Hever Castle in Kent. The medieval moated castle, the girlhood home of Queen Anne Boleyn, was bought in 1903 by William Waldorf Astor. The American financier, who settled in England in the 1890s, had for a time served as American minister in Italy and had there amassed a fine collection of classical sculptures. He made Hever a splendid retreat, restoring it to its Tudor glory and creating an exquisite Italianate garden to set off his collection. He was rewarded for his brilliant success in English society and his lavish contributions to causes with an English baronetcy.

Above Hever Castle, Kent, which became the home of William Waldorf Astor in 1903.
Left Part of the Italian garden that Astor designed for his collection of Italian sculpture.

The Heaven Room at Burghley House. Little of the original Elizabethan interior of the house survives. The main rooms were entirely redecorated during the late seventeenth century.

The Heaven Room is the masterpiece of the Italian painter Antonio Verrio who spent ten years at Burghley working on this and other rooms.

74

The Marble Hall, Holkham Hall, Norfolk. It was
designed by William Kent and is a development
on a grander scale of the sculpture gallery in
Chiswick House.

words
fail me
PLOP!

75

The central part of the south front at Hatfield House, shows how influential Italian styles were in late Renaissance England.

Even after the death of the queen in 1603, the Elizabethan age continued to cast a glow over the new reign of James, sixth of Scotland and first of England. But the panache and ebullience of the high Elizabethan era was gone. The brash and beautiful grandiloquence of a Hardwick Hall would never be repeated but the new age was not lacking in spacious and splendid houses. The prime example of the Jacobean house was built by Robert Cecil, first earl of Salisbury and son and successor in office of William Lord Burghley. King James owed much to Cecil for his smooth accession to the English crown, but he did not hesitate to force his minister to hand over the great house at Theobalds in Hertfordshire in exchange for the nearby Hatfield. Formerly belonging to the bishops of Ely, it had come to the crown during the Reformation and had served for a time as the prison of the young Elizabeth during the reign of her sister Queen Mary I. It was in the grounds of Hatfield Old Place that Elizabeth heard of her own accession as queen.

Perhaps discontented with the bargain that the king had forced on him, Robert Cecil built a new house at Hatfield. He turned to a professional architect, Robert Lyminge. Work began in 1607 and within five years the great house was complete. The pinnacles on the wing towers and the gate house towers of the central block echo Tudor motifs, but the colonnade brings classical styles to mind. Within we find a Great Hall with screen and musicians' gallery as might be expected in a Tudor house. Hatfield is on a palatial scale yet the mood, established by the mellow brick and stone of the exterior, is domestic. The interior makes provision for comforts to a quite un-Elizabethan degree: the Great Hall is there for ceremonial occasions but adjacent to it is a private dining room for more regular use. With Hatfield House, we might say, the English 'stately home' makes its first appearance.

At about the same time as Hatfield was going up, a prosperous clothier of Witney in the county of Oxfordshire, Walter Jones by name, was taking

possession of a new estate in the northern part of that county. He had bought it the previous year from Robert Catesby who, two years later, was one of the conspirators in the Gunpowder Plot against King James and Parliament. The new house that Jones built at Chastleton is one of the least changed of Jacobean manor houses, and even the gardens retain their original formal layout. The rooms, grouped round a small court, still have their fine plasterwork ceilings, fireplaces and carved wooden wainscotting, and the Great Hall also has its screen complete. The barrel-vaulted Long Gallery, patterned with roses and skirted by the original silver oak pannelling, shows how the fashions of the houses of the great were eagerly copied by the gentry. During the Civil War, the Jones family were staunch royalists and after the Battle of Worcester Robert Jones, fleeing from the royalist rout, was hidden from pursuing parliamentary troops in a secret room, while his wife and family lulled the troopers' suspicions.

Another modest country house which was built about the same time as Chastleton, was Ham House in Surrey, now in the suburbs of greater London. In the 1630s it was redecorated and enriched by William Murray, first earl of Dysart. His only child was a daughter but she was allowed to retain the title and Elizabeth, Countess of Dysart, with her second husband the Duke of Lauderdale, enlarged and extended the house. Much of the original late seventeenth-century furniture remains as it was when Elizabeth and her husband brought it to Ham. With this and the fine plasterwork of Joseph Kinsman the house is a sumptuous example of decor in the style of the Restoration period.

Above A beautiful and evocative picture of Knole House, Kent, during winter. *Above right* The exterior and saloon of Ham House, Richmond, Surrey, the home of the Lauderdales. *Right* The Great Hall of Littlecote House, Buckinghamshire. The fine collection of armour and buff coats on the walls comes from the Parliamentary forces during the Civil War.

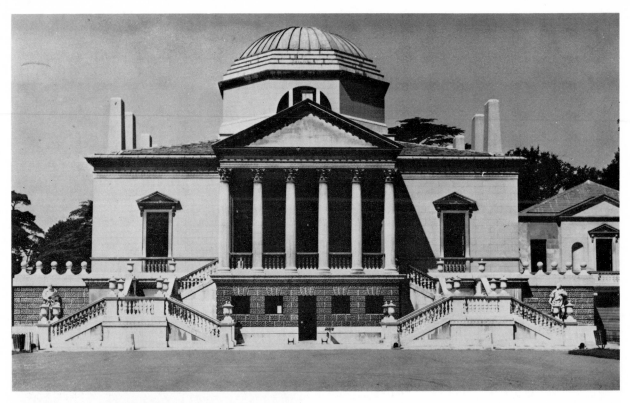

The long tradition of English gentleman-architects which began with Sir John Thynne and ran through to the nineteenth century, reached its high point with Richard Boyle, third earl of Burlington. His title came from the Yorkshire town of Burlington, now called Bridlington, and William Kent, his architect and designer, was also a native of the town. In 1725 Burlington began to build a grand new villa in the grounds of his estate at Chiswick. At first it was intended not so much to be lived in as to house the collection of sculpture and painting he had amassed in his travels to Italy. This house was to be a museum. It was inspired by the Italian Renaissance architect Palladio (1518–1580) and especially by his Villa Capra, near Vicenza, called the Rotunda. The most important room at Chiswick is the central domed hall, and the other rooms are grouped round it. The somewhat austere design was by Burlington, but some of the interior work was by Kent, and the summer parlour, which adjoins the main house, was built somewhat earlier by the Scottish architect Colen Campbell, who had given Burlington his first training in architecture.

Top Chiswick House, designed by Lord Burlington in imitation of Andrea Palladio's Rotunda at Vicenza, Italy. *Left* Sculpture Galley, Chiswick House, designed by William Kent, an idea which he developed on a grander scale at Holkham (see page 62).

At Chiswick, the three men, Burlington, Campbell and Kent launched a new movement in English architecture based on devotion to the work of Palladio. The light classical elegance of his style seems to have provided the ideal settings for the literature and philosophy of the eighteenth-century Age of Reason. Burlington's house at Chiswick became the shrine of Palladianism and a gathering place of writers and artists under his patronage.

By the end of the 1730s, the Palladian style was the only fashionable one for a new house and its first important successor was Holkham Hall in Norfolk. The site, owned by a young man called Thomas Coke, was for the most part sand dunes and salty marshes. When he was only fifteen, Coke had set out on the Grand Tour of Europe, an indispensable part of the education of any English gentleman at that time. He spent much of his time in Italy, where he met Burlington and Kent. He returned to England at the age of twenty-one, fired by the dream of a villa in the Roman style at Holkham. But it was only in 1734, when he was thirty-seven, that work was begun. Kent was the architect and at Holkham he developed some of the features of Chiswick on a larger scale; the most striking instance is the sculpture hall.

Houses all over England were soon being built in the classical idiom or remodelled to suit the new fashion, but few can match the simple and elegant statement achieved by Robert Adam at Osterley Park. The original house on the site had been built for the Elizabethan founder of the Royal Exchange in London, Sir Thomas Gresham. In 1711 it was bought by a rich banker, Sir Francis Child, and it was for his descendants that Adam converted the Tudor mansion into a 'palace of palaces.' The first plan was to rebuild entirely, but instead the old place was given a face lift. The principal rooms were shifted up to the first floor and the entrance was redesigned in a spectacular classical colonnaded portico with a lordly flight of marble stairs.

Top Holkham Hall, Norfolk, home of the Earl of Leicester. *Above* Osterley Park, Middlesex, as it was redesigned by Robert Adam in the early eighteenth century.

Osterley was Adam's masterpiece as an architect and much of the furniture was also designed by him. The result is an exquisite monument to the Age of Reason. In the next century the English tradition of taking continental or exotic styles and adapting them to local conditions took a new direction. The search for inspiration now reached back into time. The taste for medievalism had never really died. Even in the middle of the eighteenth century, Horace Walpole, writer and statesman, had converted his residence at Strawberry Hill, Richmond, with a riot of medievalising fantasy, and towards the end of the century the taste for things 'Gothick' became a craze. It continued into the nineteenth century, in competition with the still strong impulse towards classicism, and both trends, although so different in effect, expressed a perennial European tendency to dress the buildings of the present in the styles of the past.

Top left The 'Estruscan' style was fashionable during the eighteenth century; this beautiful room is at Osterley. *Top right* The Long Gallery, Strawberry Hill, Twickenham, where Horace Walpole indulged his fancy for the 'Gothick'.

Left Chartwell, the home of Sir Winston Churchill.
Bottom left William Beckford's 'Gothick' extravaganza Fonthill Abbey, in Wiltshire.
Below Belvoir Castle, Leicestershire, home of the Duke of Rutland, was rebuilt in splendidly medieval style in the early nineteenth century.

Early Victorian Gothic revivalism was heralded by the fantastic Abbey at Fonthill, built for the eccentric Samuel Beckett. The architect, James Wyatt, worked closely to the requirements of his rich employer and the outcome was one of the strangest houses ever seen in England. Its slender and lofty spire was the subject of astonishment and a good deal of ridicule. Its collapse within ten years of its completion caused a good deal of satisfaction to the critics. Beckett's only reaction was bitter disappointment that he had not been at Fonthill to see the disaster.

The romantic nostalgia for the middle ages which made the historical novels of Sir Walter Scott best sellers, achieved one of its finest moments at Belvoir Castle, the home of the dukes of Rutland. It was the third castle on the site, originally occupied in the eleventh century. The architect was James Wyatt. A fire ravaged the new buildings in 1816 but building continued, thanks to the determination of Elizabeth, the fifth duchess. The Elizabeth Saloon, called after her, is decorated throughout in the rococo taste of the court of Louis XV of France. It set a fashion. Belvoir broke new ground in another direction. The quest for variety in historical styles reached

such a pitch that different rooms were decorated in different styles: the grand dining room was Norman baronial, another suite was hung with Chinese wall papers, and so on. In 1813 the Prince Regent visited the castle and the Regent Suite was specially prepared and decorated for the occasion. As the industrial revolution remorselessly upturned the life-patterns of generations, men looked for security in reconstructing the past.

Above The Elizabeth Room at Belvoir Castle. As the nineteenth century progressed great houses had various rooms redesigned in different historic styles. This room at Belvoir, designed for Elizabeth the fifth duchess in the style of Louis XV in France, was one of the first.
Opposite Disraeli's library in his home at Hughenden Manor, near High Wycombe, Buckinghamshire.

At Hughenden Manor, the home of Benjamin Disraeli, the great prime minister, the research into history came full circle. The house was a Georgian one built in the 1780s but Disraeli, fascinated by everything Tudor, had it redesigned in the style of the first great age of English house building.

One of the most remarkable residences in England is tucked away in the Buckinghamshire countryside, not far from Hughenden. Today, Claydon House is only of middling size, while the fine west façade is of a restrained classicism. But inside the house is a riot of fancy.

The Verney family took over the lease on the house from one of their tenants in 1620. The late medieval building remained unchanged during most of the seventeenth century for the Verneys, divided by the Civil War between king and parliament, had a checkered career. The father, Sir Edmund, was one of the most romantic and remarkable figures in that heroic period of English history. Although he had been in the royal service throughout his life, when the Civil War broke out his political and religious sympathies were entirely parliamentarian. Nevertheless his fierce personal sense of honour held him loyal to the king. 'I have eaten his bread,' he wrote, 'served

him for near thirty years, and I will not do so base a thing as to forsake him, but choose rather to lose my life (which I am sure I shall do) to preserve and defend those things which are against my conscience to preserve and defend.' He died at Edgehill and after the battle his severed hand was found grasping the royal standard.

Claydon today is a diminished monument to the imagination and ambitions of Ralph, second earl of Verney, who died in 1791. He was a quixotic figure, his coach and six always escorted by outriders, a 'brace of tall negroes, with silver French horns . . . perpetually making a noise,' but he was also devoted to the arts and culpably generous to his friends. Worst of all, his neighbour was a wealthy political rival and he felt bound to outdo him in his architectural schemes. He bankrupted himself in the process. Verney inherited the handsome but unremarkable Tudor manor house. In 1754 he added the large stable court. Next he extended the south front of the house and then turned his attention to the west. The new front when complete stretched more than 250 feet, but within years of Earl Ralph's death much of it was demolished, so that the handsome façade that today looks out over the lakes is only half the size it once was.

For architects, Verney had Sir Thomas Robinson, an eccentric Yorkshire country gentleman and amateur architect, and a local craftsman and master-builder named Luke Lightfoot. The work on the house was a history of conflict, ill-feeling and recrimination. The focus was first Lightfoot's fantastic chinoiserie designs for the interior. Robinson won the first round, displacing the local genius with his own nominee, the renowned plaster stuccoist, Joseph Rose, who had worked with Robert Adam on Osterley House. Lightfoot's dismissal was not only a matter of taste, Lord Verney also took him to law for embezzling some £20,000 and objected equally to his cavalier attitude to social rank. On one occasion he received his patron 'with his hat on his head . . . and did not ask me to sit down.' Like Verney himself and Robinson, Lightfoot was certainly an eccentric. He was also immensely talented and produced an astounding series of rococo decorations, which reach their climax in the Chinese Room.

Not the least remarkable feature of the work is the fact that it is in wood. Such intricate effects were usually achieved with moulded stucco, much easier to work. The designs themselves are mainly taken from the architects' and designers' pattern books published in London, but Lightfoot's virtuosity in producing them at all is phenomenal. More breathtaking even than this exquisite fantasy is the staircase in the centre of the house. The plaster work on the walls and ceiling is by Joseph Rose. It is superbly done but it is quite eclipsed by the stairs and the balustrade. The two flights of stairs are completely encased in minutely worked wood inlay. The geometric designs on the treads and risers are echoed by similar work on the underside of the case. The visitor today must make his way up the building on a specially built second staircase so that the masterpiece in the main hall may be preserved. For it is not only the inlay work that is so precious. The balustrade is a miracle of wrought iron in which leaves and ears of corn sway and rustle.

For all the richness of its decorations, Claydon is very much a house for living in. The room of Florence Nightingale, who stayed there on many occasions, epitomises the air of domesticity that still clings to the place, while the setting of the house in its rolling landscaped grounds gives an air of informal identity with the countryside which was the characteristic aim of the English style of garden. From the greatest to the least, the houses we have looked at in this chapter were the homes of private gentlemen. A simple house, like the one in which the poet Keats lived in Hampstead, had this in common even with a great palace like Blenheim, that they were both owned by subjects of the same monarch, both Englishmen and both subject to the same law.

Top left The west front of Claydon House, Buckinghamshire, a truly prime example of the classic style of the English country house.
Bottom left The inlaid staircase at Claydon.
Above The alcove in the remarkable Chinese room at Claydon.

The Residence of Princes

From the early sixteenth century onwards, the wealth of Europe increased dramatically as its commerce stretched ever further into the outside world. The voyages around Africa in the previous century and above all the discovery of the riches of southern and central America brought a fabulous influx of wealth in luxury articles and specie. Much of this new-found wealth went naturally to finance war–the ambitions of the Spanish Habsburgs and the conflicts between Catholic and Protestant that rumbled across the continent for more than a hundred years–but much of it found its way into the coffers of princes, and the hands of new families rising in the world through trade, and to the papal treasury. In an age when ostentation and display were an important measure of power and prestige, and the canons of taste were secure in a common respect for learning and beauty, building and the decorative arts flourished on an unprecedented scale and in a quality that has become a part of the western heritage.

The vast majority of the houses in this chapter were built between 1500 and 1800, between the age of humanism and the age of elegance. Fashions changed but throughout this long period the basic inspiration of European architecture came from the rediscovery of classical models during the Renaissance, and the decorative arts were devoted to essentially naturalistic concepts. The result, to the modern eye, is one of surprising homogeneity. The style of the beautiful little mansion at Malmaison, renovated for Napoleon and Josephine in the early 1800s, is yet another reinterpretation of the classical idiom first proclaimed in the villas and palazzi of Italian princes and prelates three hundred years earlier.

The Roman villa, to the ancient Italians a charming residence, had been an important factor in civilising the peoples that they conquered to the north. In the unsettled times that followed the collapse of the Empire, some villas became centres for new towns, some became fortified residences but most fell into decay. During the middle ages the characteristic residence of the great man was a castle rather than a house, but in Italy signs of a new, more domestic kind of accommodation, began to emerge as early as 1200.

The bedroom of the Empress Josephine at Malmaison.

This would be a good resting place in your ark room —

Even so it was the medieval castle that often provided the model for the ground plan for the earliest villas of the Renaissance. Many villas of the fourteenth and fifteenth centuries had strong walls, small windows and sometimes battlements and towers.

In the cramped space within the city walls there was little room for great mansions, but in the *contado*, the countryside surrounding a town, fine houses with gardens were built and began to acquire a distinctive architectural style. In the sixteenth century, the villas built by the princes of the Church around Rome had gardens that were integrated with the house and not only in æsthetic terms; porches, colonnades and stairways broke the garden landscape and offered tempting walks.

These new Roman villas, like the Villa d'Este or the Villa Farnese, were built on hill sites commanding fine views of the surrounding countryside and their façades are often rich in the contrasts of light and shade produced by the colonnades and recesses of windows and porches.

A characteristic of the new Italian houses was the placing of the main rooms on the first floor called the *piano nobile* or the 'grand level'. In this type of house, the ground floor was used for storage, kitchens and perhaps servants' quarters, where the windows were often fewer and smaller than in the upper storeys.

A fine example of a great house built with protection as well as comfort in mind is the Villa Farnese. It stands on the summit of a hill, a site once occupied by a castle, outside the village of Caprarola, in the well-wooded range of mountains called the Monti Cimini. Some thirty-five miles to the south-east is Rome. Designed by the architect Vignola, the palace was begun in 1550 for Cardinal Alessandro Farnese. The grandson of Pope Paul III, the Cardinal belonged to a family that the new pope, Julius III, was determined to humiliate. Caprarola lay in the Farnese family estates and the bleak landscape and strong site made for an easily defensible position.

The architecture of the massive fortress-like building is austere in the extreme and its semi-military air is emphasised by the five bastions, one at each corner, which support the platform on which the palace stands. The pentagonal ground plan is the more unusual because within is a great circular courtyard. The place is approached by a series of staircases sweeping across the front of the façade and taking in a large esplanade, where the Cardinal's private troop of horse exercised. Undoubtedly the Villa Farnese

had a serious military purpose but behind its gaunt walls it is truly palatial both in extent and decorations.

The services, kitchens and store rooms, were housed in a basement storey excavated from the rock, but above this are the great rooms and halls of the state apartments. One of the grandest is the Hall of Annals, a rectangular room lavishly decorated by the Zuccaro brothers with scenes from the history of the Farnese family. Perhaps the most startling feature of the place is a magnificent spiral staircase which rises three storeys and is a monumental conception. The stairs are carried on pairs of Ionic columns and the whole is decorated with frescoes and cartouches and allegorical subjects.

Even in the spacious and elaborate gardens, the military theme finds an echo, for the lower garden is divided from the house by a drawbridge. Behind the garden rises a wooded slope which brings the visitor to one of the most admired parts of the whole palace. This is the casino built for one of the Cardinal's successors. Today it is an official residence for the President of Italy and its setting certainly makes it an imposing home for a head of state. It is fronted by a colonnaded loggia and below this, from a grotto guarded by two huge river gods, a cascade of water flows down between rusticated arches to a fountain.

Top The main façade of the Villa Farnese. *Above* The casino at Caprarola seen from the gardens. *Right* A corner of the formal garden, or parterre, that lies below the casino.

90

During the second half of the sixteenth century, the hills about Rome were alive with building activity. The great princes of the Church began to vie with one another in the splendour of their out-of-town villas. The private charms of the Villa Lante are delightful, especially because they are unusual. It is a place of enchantment which seems to bewitch everyone who sees it. For one writer this little house sums up everything that is best in the western tradition of domestic architecture. It lies secretly on a hillside in the range of the Monti Cimini, near the town of Viterbo. It has none of the grandiose manners of so many other Italian villas, but combines rich domestic comforts with a love of gardens in a truly unique blend.

Thanks to the devoted and fine restoration by its modern owner, Villa Lante looks today much as it did in the late sixteenth century when the designs of its founder, Cardinal Gianfrancesco Gambara, were completed. Appointed as the chief ecclesiastical dignitary of Viterbo in 1566, he at once began work on a villa outside the village of Bagnaia. Strangely, the architect of this gem among Renaissance houses is not known for sure, but it seems likely that the idea for its unique design originated with the cardinal himself. It was certainly his most cherished possession.

It is approached from a small piazza at the top end of the village of Bagnaia through an unpretentious arch. This leads into the lower garden of the villa, the Quadrato. The centre of interest is not the house but a beautiful and elaborate fountain consisting of four classical youths holding aloft a device surmounted by a star, from which shoots the jets of the fountain. Through the centuries the salts in the water have blackened the statues so that the fountain has long been known as the Fountain of the Moors. It is surrounded by water gardens and formal beds in which box hedges are laid out in geometrical patterns.

Comparison of the eighteenth century engraving of the Villa Lante with the modern photograph *(opposite)* shows how completely the house is preserved.

This should be a little past-time
for you in your spare moments!
all of you Git Busy — damn it Jorit

to get lost in the maze (or something) when I come a-visiting

93

The Fountain of the Moors, Villa Lante.

This and the other fountains and waterworks in the gardens are fed by a stream which flows from high up the mountainside into the garden at its upper end. This is quite densely wooded so that the little stream enters the boundaries of the garden in a contrived 'natural' environment. As the water makes its way down the hill, towards the Quadrato, the layout of the gardens becomes more and more formal as if to stress, in conformity with Renaissance theories, that the natural meanders of the stream are being disciplined to serve the designs of the gardener. The splash of the water is heard everywhere and the glint of the fountains and pools create the magic of the place. But the most remarkable fact about the Villa Lante is that it is not one but two houses. Between the Upper Garden and the Quadrato stand two identical pavilions. The one on the right as we look up the garden, was built by Gambara at the same time as he completed the Quadrato and the Upper Garden. Work was then suspended. But we know that the idea of the two pavilions was his from a fresco in the Gambara pavilion, showing the villa as it was intended. The second pavilion was built by his successor, Cardinal Peretti di Montalato.

Both Caprarola and Viterbo are comparatively remote from Rome. Nearer to hand, only about twenty miles to the north east, is the hillside town of Tivoli. Once again the visitor finds himself in a piazza of the town with a doorway that invites investigation. On the other side of it he is in the grounds of another of the myriad pleasure villas of Renaissance Italy.

Tivoli, on the hills that skirt the plain in which Rome stands, had been a favoured site during classical times. The ruins of the Emperor Hadrian's villa can still be seen. But when the architect Pirro Ligorio began work in 1550 on the new house commissioned by Cardinal Ippolito d'Este, the new fashion for the place had barely begun. Like Gambara, he was in the papal administration, governor of the town of Tivoli; like Farnese, he too traced his descent from a previous pope. Unlike them, he had had serious hopes of the papal throne itself, stemming as he did on his father's side from one of the oldest princely houses in Italy. His new villa provided a retreat from the world of politics where his ambitions had in fact been thwarted.

The villa was also a place on which the cardinal could show his patronage of the arts. It took ten years to build, but the paintings and other decorations took twice that time to complete. The architecture of the façade is plain but the treasures within are matched by the gardens, which are the most renowned of Renaissance Italy. From the house one looks down over the plain towards Rome, across the trees and terraces of the garden. Water is everywhere. The Way of the Hundred Fountains stretches across the full width of the garden. It is skirted by a wide terrace and from the centre of this the central axis of the garden sweeps down the hill side round the Fountain of the Dragons. This is said to have been built in a single night to honour the sudden arrival of a pope whose arms included the dragon.

From these villas of great princes of the Church we turn to a palace built for a great secular aristocrat. The ducal palace of Urbino, a hill town in Umbria, northern Italy, is largely the conception of Federigo da Montefeltro. He reigned as Duke of Urbino from 1444 to 1482, a popular and munificent ruler. Though he kept one of the most renowned and civilized courts in Italy, the little state's income depended not on trade but on warfare. In the unending and complicated struggles of fifteenth-century Italy, the profession of soldier was both profitable and necessary. The merchants who ruled most of the great cities did not have the love of war that drove

Even the ruins of the Emperor Hadrian's villa at Tivoli are a place of enchantment. After the decline of the empire, Tivoli had to wait a thousand years to become yet again a fashionable retreat outside Rome.

Pick out all the statues you like —
But Beware of frisbee "Bad aeneas!"

the aristocrat out to battle. Instead they hired private mercenary armies, commanded by a hardy breed of adventurers called *condottiere*. The more successful could rise from humble beginnings to the nobility itself. Others, like Duke Federigo, were born aristocrats who made warfare their livelihood.

Urbino had been in his family for 300 years and its hill site was an ideal base for a military commander. Until his time, the ducal residence had been a fortress. He had it re-designed as a palace. He commissioned his architect, Laurana, to build a 'fair residence befitting our rank and reputation and that of our predecessors.' It was also, in conformity with Renaissance ideals of the great dwelling, to be a 'city within a city.' In buildings like this, the house reached the last frontier of its development. Built to the request of one man to house himself and his family, it had also, as 'befitted his rank' to provide accommodation for a household of 350 people and more than 300 horses.

Above and right The ducal palace at Urbino and the duke's bedroom.

At the heart of the palatial apartments is the most beautiful room of all. This is the private study of the duke, decorated throughout with the most exquisite inlay in many-coloured woods, to designs by the great artist Botticelli. With cunning effects of illusionist perspective, the flat walls seem to be lined with deep cupboards and shelves, crowded with books and scientific and musical instruments. One of the most fascinating and gifted men of Renaissance Italy, Duke Federigo was a true scholar and his library, housed in two rooms in a place of honour either side of the entrance courtyard, was claimed to have been finer than the one in Florence. The palace became a home of humanist studies and of art, poetry and mathematics. The shimmering towers and turrets of the huge palace dominate the town and remind the modern visitor of its military past. Within, the light, airy and graceful halls and rooms are the perfect setting for a great Renaissance court.

Below The duke's private salon—originally the cold walls would have been covered with tapestries. *Bottom* Duke Federigo's study at Urbino, despite appearances the walls are entirely flat but covered with exquisite marquetry.

Wall paintings were a common form of
decoration from the middle ages through to the
eighteenth century. The magnificent Heaven
Room at Burghley House, England (page 63) is
a fine example of the later stage of the art.
Opposite top An early example of wall painting
from the medieval Palazzo Davanzati, Florence.
Opposite bottom The gardens of the Villa d'Este,
the most magnificent, perhaps, among the many
magnificent gardens in Italy. *Above* The superb
Hall of the Annals at the Villa Farnese by the
Zuccaro brothers. From floor to ceiling the
room is lined with the story of the family of the
builder of the villa. *Left* A glimpse of the
cascade in the gardens of the Villa Farnese,
Caprarola.

Below Formal gardens above the landing stage at the palace island of Isola Bella. *Bottom* The palace seen from Stresa across Lake Maggiore; foothills of the Alps can be seen in the background. *Opposite* The great fountain in the grounds at Isola Bella.

The last of the Italian houses to be surveyed, Isola Bella, took three hundred years to build, being begun in the seventeenth century and completed only in our own. It is situated on one of the islands in Lake Maggiore, owned by the princely Borromeo family. Like most other great houses these days, Isola Bella has been thrown open to the public, but there is a difference. The revenue was originally intended simply to meet the running costs of the place yet, in a very short time, enough was raised to finish the building as it had been planned generations earlier. The house is surrounded by other islands whose inhabitants are all tenants of the great family and feel an almost proprietorial pride in the great establishment in their midst. Today, this dream island palace, which entranced Alexandre Dumas and Richard Wagner, stands complete like a romance from another age to bewitch our more prosaic generation.

PWL — contemplating just how
He'll modernise this masterpiece!

Right Behind the cascade is the casino of the Villa Farnese, Caprarola. *Below* The Palazzo Contarini del Bovolo in Venice. The magnificent staircase served a very practical purpose being the only connecting link between the different floors. Since the ground floor was usually occupied by tradesmen and the top floors by poor lodgers, the family on the middle floor had to protect its privacy as best it could. *Opposite* The Amber Palace, India. The formal gardens of this Moslem mansion have surprising similarities of mood with the geometric designs of Italian Renaissance gardens.

The Italy of the Renaissance and for centuries to come, was divided between a number of principalities and powers. They range from small territories like that of the dukes of Urbino to the rich and dazzling might of Venice whose maritime empire stretched down the Adriatic to the Aegean sea. It was in these flourishing and independent states that the merchant class of Europe first came into its own. In the great northern kingdom of France, even in the seventeenth century, the high road to riches and prestige still lay through the offices of the royal court. Formal salaries were not over large but the opportunities open to officers of state to line their own pockets out of the revenues of their departments were immense. In fact they constituted the chief attraction of the royal service to most ambitious men. The houses we turn to all belong to this century and were all built on this kind of money. Today they appear as part of a proud national heritage, but even when they were built they were seen by some as the fruits of corruption.

In 1642, Michel Particelli d'Émery, the Intendant of the Royal Finances, bought a great castle from the Coligny d'Andelot family. They descended from Gaspard de Goligny, Admiral of France, who was one of the first Protestants to be assassinated in the massacre of the Huguenots on St Bartholomew's Eve. The room where he and his ardent Protestant brothers used to meet can still be seen. The four-square fortress with its round corner towers, which provided the basis of d'Émery's new mansion, was transformed by the genius of his architect into the beautiful Château de Tanlay that we see today. The château is still surrounded by a moat, sixty feet wide and filled with clean water from a specially constructed canal which the architect incorporated in the design of the grounds. The approach to the great court is over a fine stone bridge and through a gatehouse.

The Château de Tanlay was completed in 1648, the very year in which Cardinal Mazarin, regent for the child king, Louis XIV, dismissed d'Émery. He had show considerable ingenuity in creating new debts to liquidate the old, inventing new offices to sell and reviving ancient taxes. One of these was derived from an edict dating from the Hundred Years War against England which had forbidden the building of houses in the zone surrounding the walls of Paris, on military grounds. It had been long forgotten and flourishing suburbs had sprung up. D'Émery's department

proposed a levy on all these 'illegal' houses, though many had stood for generations. It was this kind of thing, as much as his 'borrowings' from the royal revenue, that caused his dismissal. He was sacked as a political precaution because of popular pressure against his tricks of revenue raising. He had kept his corruption within the bounds thought reasonable during the Regency and he was left to enjoy his fortune in the retirement and peace of his new château. His sister married into the de Tanlay family, who still own the great house.

104

Opposite The moat and entrance façade to the Château de Tanlay. *Above* Tanlay from the gardens.

P.S. *measuring out on the jobs to roll a Hoop!*

The Château de Valençay, France, where the
great nineteenth century statesman Talleyrand
lived.

An interior in the Hôtel Lambert, Paris. For generations the great house was derelict or being used for storage and similar purposes. It has been carefully restored and the solid mid-seventeenth century French furniture restores the air of opulent and solid grandeur.

The glorious achievements of Italian architecture had a deep working effect throughout Europe and their influence is apparent in Le Vau's work. The pilasters and portico of the façade and the balustrades in the garden are obvious examples of this and there are many more, but the steeply pitched roofs are in the traditional French style. The formal gardens with their strictly geometrical patterns, show how the logical French mind reinterpreted the art of the Italian garden to produce an entirely new concept.

Three whole villages had to be razed to the ground to clear the way for the vast grounds at Vaux-le-Vicomte. The pavements in the grounds and the panelling of the apartments were completed in little more than a year and within five years, as we have seen, the palace was complete. During the eighteenth century, Vaux went through the hands of a succession of owners and had a chequered career, but in the 1870s it was restored to its original glories and today, still in private hands, it is one of the most magnificent great houses in the whole of France.

Nicolas Fouquet, Superintendant of the Royal Finances in the 1650s, was not to have the good fortune of d'Émery. In 1661 he received the 23-year-old Louis XIV at his palace of Vaux-le-Vicomte. It was an occasion of the most dazzling festivities and these may well have been a major mistake. Fouquet's ostentatious wealth had already earned him many enemies and the young Louis was bitter at the comparative poverty of his own court when set against the state maintained by his great minister. Within two weeks of the king's departure, Fouquet was arrested and imprisoned. He remained in captivity for the rest of his life and his splendid mansion, though eventually returned to his wife, was maliciously plundered by the king. Trees were uprooted and transported to Versailles and the brilliant group of artists and designers were taken into the royal service to work on the great palace which was intended to overshadow Vaux-le-Vicomte completely.

The men that Louis took over from his hated minister were mostly in their late thirties and early forties and had successful careers behind them. André Le Nôtre was probably the greatest of all French garden designers, Charles Le Brun was a gifted artist and a master of organising large scale decorative schemes and the architect was Louis Le Vau who, besides Vaux-le-Vicomte had already designed the magnificent Hôtel Lambert in Paris. Even the great Nicolas Poussin, the grand old man of French painting, had worked at Vaux.

The Hôtel Lambert, which had brought Louis Le Vau fame as an architect, stands on the Ile St Louis in the centre of Paris. At the time of its building, the island was barely inhabited. The transformation owed much to Jean-Baptiste, Lambert, secretary to the young Louis XIV. He died in the 1640s and his brother, Nicolas, inherited the palace. His wealth was so great that when he was later fined a million livres by the king for his involvement in the corruption surrounding the Fouquet affair, he not only paid up but continued to enjoy his nick-name of Lambert the Rich. Ten years later he was president of the Royal Chamber of Accounts.

It was at the Hôtel Lambert that Charles Le Brun, like Le Vau, achieved his first great commission and indeed perhaps his best. The Gallery of the Apotheosis of Hercules shows a fluency and lightness of touch that was to become stilted in formality when he came to work for the King at Versailles. The entrance to the palace itself is up a staircase flanked by classical columns. At ground level the main courtyard is surrounded by kitchens, stables and storehouses. Inside, a magnificent staircase takes the visitor up to an oval vestibule off which open the grand state apartments. The influence of Italian models is apparent but the dignified restraint of the age of Louis XIV give the the house its style. After Nicolas Lambert in 1692, the palace passed to a succession of owners. In the late eighteenth century the collection of art treasures was sold off. During the early 1800s it was for a time a girls' boarding school and even a military storehouse. During the twentieth century, however, the grand apartments have been restored and we can once again feel something of their original opulence.

During the seventeenth century, France became the major power in Europe. She was ruled by an autocratic sovereign who established his ascendancy over the proudest and most unruly aristocracy, and built his power on the talents of a body of new men who earned their wealth in the service of the king and built their great houses on the proceeds of this service. They were not independent princes but they lived in houses that had the scale of palaces. Across the Rhine, this grandeur was being imitated by men of like wealth and ambitions who, however, ruled their own territories.

From the middle ages to the nineteenth century, the German-speaking lands of central and northern Europe were divided among scores of small states and cities. To the south lay the extensive Habsburg domains and in the north-east was the electorate of Brandenburg, later to grow into the kingdom of Prussia, and become the dominant power. In the 1720s, the prince-bishops of Würzburg were among the numerous noble families ruling autonomous territories that yielded a sizeable revenue. Like others, they used their money in lavish building projects.

It was in the year 1720 that a new chief palace for the prince-bishopric was begun by Count Johann-Philipp-Franz von Schönborn, who had been appointed bishop the year before. The work was to last another twenty years after the death of Count Johann-Philipp in 1724. During those years a galaxy of talented architects and artists from Austria, Italy and Switzerland as well as from Germany were at work. The masterplan was drawn up by Balthasar Neumann, who from humble beginnings rose, under the patronage of the prince-bishop, to be the greatest figure in the whole magnificent movement of eighteenth-century German architecture. The great frontage was to stretch 550 feet.

Top left The mansion of Vaux-le-Vicomte from the gardens to the south. *Above* The Oval Salon at Vaux-le-Vicomte, designed by Louis Le Vau.

A beautiful view of the gardens at
Vaux-le-Vicomte through the window of a
handsome painted wood panelled room.

The Library at Vaux-le-Vicomte now furnished
with the comfortable upholstery of the
nineteenth and twentieth centuries.

In its vast size and breath-taking drama, the Residenz at Würzburg is one of the most glorious palaces in Europe. It is certainly the masterpiece of the German rococo style. The first staggering view of the façade prepares the visitor to expect splendour. The entrance hall, a forest of pillars supporting the staircase, holds back the visitor's expectancy in an air of mystery, but mounting the staircase reveals one of the most astonishing achievements of eighteenth-century art. It is the ceiling of the staircase painted by the Venetian artist Giambattista Tiepolo. He had won a European reputation with his frescoes in Venice and in 1750 he was invited to Würzburg, there he worked for three years. The ceiling, which spans a vast area, symbolises on its four sides the four continents of the then known world, Europe, Asia, Africa and America and in the sky between them float the personifications of the planets. The whole allegorical scheme is composed of hundreds of figures, organised with brilliant effect

and alive with the lightness of Tiepolo's style.

In the place of honour at the stairhead is a tableau representing Europe. On the cornice reclines the architect Balthasar Neumann himself, with a faithful hunting dog, and above his head floats a medallion portrait of the prince-bishop, Karl Philipp von Greiffenclau who commissioned Tiepolo. The artist's other masterpiece in the Residenz is the Kaisersaal ceiling. Here the portraits include that of the medieval emperor Frederick Barbarossa and over them all the horse-drawn chariot of the sun god Apollo soars across the sky.

Above The Tiepolo ceiling in the staircase hall at the Residenz, Würzburg.

Count von Schönborn's uncle, Lothar-Franz von Schönborn, the bishop of neighbouring Bamberg, was a still more prolific builder. Outside the beautiful mid-German town stands his great house of Pommersfelden, built in the 1710s. The stables alone make a magnificent building that is almost a palace in itself. Within, the mansion is a riot of rococo sculpture, columns and decorations. As at Würzburg, the staircase is one of the great features and the richly marbled and inlaid floors and the lavishly decorated ceilings give the place, still owned by the family of its founder, the delightful atmosphere of a palace in the heyday of the german principalities.

Top left The Chapel at Würzburg.
Top right The staircase hall at Pommersfelden, one of the finest achievements of the German baroque. *Right* The south entrance, Pommersfelden.

This epoch in German history, which saw the building of a cluster of architectural masterpieces, the blossoming of the German tradition of music in Bach, Handel, Haydn and Mozart, was the age of Goethe, Schiller and other great writers, and drew to a close in the turmoil of the Napoleonic wars. The campaigns of French and other foreign armies forced the Germans to think in terms of unity and during the nineteenth century the movement gathered momentum. It came to fruition in 1870 with the proclamation of the Prussian king as emperor of Germany. Until Napoleon, the greatest power in Germany had been the empire of the Habsburgs, but Austria never fully recovered its prestige after the defeats inflicted by the French, and gradually the lead passed to Prussia. This young state first achieved the stature of a European power during the reign of Frederick II called 'the Great', remembered by later generations as the 'founder of Prussian militarism'. Undoubtedly an effective military commander, he was also a man of cosmopolitan culture, a musician and composer of parts, a patron of Voltaire and a considerable patron of architecture.

The architect in charge was Georg Wenzelaus von Knobelsdorff, but a pencil sketch by the king of the curving terraces of the garden front as they were to be built shows that he himself had a hand in the design. The main façade is lined with suitably impressive colonnades of classical pillars, but the rooms of the palace within reveal it for what it was meant to be, an elegant and semi-domestic retreat from the cares of state–the very name is the French for 'free from care'. The scheme of decoration represents one of the most successful achievements of the rococo style. The sinuous line and the light and elegant motifs contrast happily with the formalism of the entrance, while the fantastic Chinese pavilion in the grounds, ringed by sculpture of 'Chinese' style figures, is the culmination of the European fashion for chinoiserie.

German rococo style grew from an original Italian idea grafted on to the French metamorphosis of that idea, and the result was a new theme, specific to European art. If Germany was somewhat remote from direct Italian influence, and German architecture during the eighteenth century was less obviously derived from Italian inspiration than was the French, still more remote from the Italian experience was the architecture of Spain.

Opposite page Frederick the Great had the name of his palace of Sans Souci at Potsdam inscribed over the windows of the central pavilion on the south front. *Left* The dome of the Chinese tea house Sans Souci.

Top The dome room at Benrath which links the two garden rooms. *Above* The palace of Benrath from across the lake.

The Casa de Pilatos stands in the centre of Seville. It was built by Enriques de Ribera, the first Marquis of Tarifa, after his return from a visit to the Holy Land in the early sixteenth century. It was popularly believed that he had modelled it on the house of Pilate in Jerusalem. Built two and a half centuries after the Moors had been expelled from Seville, the house is nevertheless in Moorish style. It presents a blank and uninteresting façade to the street and, set in the midst of a maze of winding streets, it reveals nothing of its delights to the outside world, but within it is a charming and private world of courtyards and cool, shady rooms. The street entrance is unimposing and the true entrance, across a small courtyard, is a fine rounded arch, Romanesque in shape but decorated with Moorish designs. The fashions for this light and sophisticated decoration lingered long in southern Spain, as though in subconscious homage to the deeply civilising effect of the five hundred years of Islamic culture.

The main courtyard of the Casa de Pilatos is surrounded by a colonnaded cloister and the ancient Roman statuary that decorates it makes an unexpected contrast to the Moorish decoration that covers the court as it does the rest of the house. The most remarkable feature of the place is the tiled staircase. Four wide flights take the visitor up to a gallery that runs round the courtyard at first floor level. The staircase is one of the most outstanding examples of tiling anywhere in the world, and makes an overpoweringly lavish effect. Typical of the Moorish style that it so faithfully copies, the Casa de Pilatos offers the visitor unexpected views into courtyards and gardens.

The house is a haven of shade under the burning Spanish sun and, withdrawn from the bustle of the streets, it provides quiet retreat from the city even though it stands at its heart. During its heyday it was an important centre for artists. Many came from the surrounding towns to copy the Roman statuary.

The courtyard house, turning in on itself from the outside world so that windows are shaded by courtyards and colonnades, has been a part of the city scene ever since ancient times. It is the natural type for lands of hot climate, being characteristic of the great Arab cities of the past and there are many other examples in the towns of southern Spain, such as the house of El Greco at Toledo.

The grand Palacio Liria, the town house of the Dukes of Alba, only a short distance from the Plaza de España in the heart of Madrid, is from a different world. Begun in 1770, it is a proud example of late baroque. The rustication on the ground floor is surmounted by a façade articulated by classical columns and pilasters. Set back from the pediment which stretches the length of the building are the windows of the third floor rooms. In the middle of the front and back façades rise stone pediments surmounted by classical urns at the back and at the front by the arms of the Alba family. The palace houses one of the world's most magnificent private collections of paintings, among them Titian's portrait of the great Duke of Alba who commanded the armies of the Emperor Charles V during the sixteenth century and also the portrait of the Duchess of Alba by Goya.

The Moorish courtyard of the Casa de Pilatos (*opposite page*) is, a little unexpectedly, also embellished with classical statues. *Top right* A view into the courtyard, Casa de Pilatos. *Above* Garden front, Palacio Liria, Madrid. *Right* Goya's portrait of the Duchess of Alba, who lived in the Palacio Liria.

Most of the houses discussed in this chapter have been grand palaces set in spacious grounds, but there are many hundreds of fine houses in the towns of Europe behind apparently modest façades. In the commercial cities of the Low Countries, where space was at a high premium, the wealthy merchant classes built high-rise mansions, often beautiful examples of the architect's art and luxuriously furnished within. Interestingly, however, one of the last grand European town palaces was built in the Belgian capital of Brussels: the Palais Stoclet. For all its modernistic idiom of design, it was in the great European tradition. There have been comparatively few mansions of such confidence and scale built in Europe during this century.

In house building as in every other department, modern European architecture has been marked by experiment and adventure. It has cut loose from conventional ideas of 'the living space' partitioned into separate rooms and designed for a life style in which social distinctions were important and the home had to accommodate various types of formal activity. The freer life style of our time, coupled with the invention of new building materials and heating and lighting systems has given the home designer the widest possible scope for building spaces that are practical, comfortable, versatile and relaxed.

Above El Greco's house at Toledo.

Top The famous House of Shells in Salamanca, Spain, is almost the symbol of the town.

Left The 'Glass House', Cologne, designed by the German architect, Bruno Taut (1914).
Below and bottom The Villa Laroche in Paris, designed by Le Corbusier for his brother Albert Jeanneret and M. La Roche, was one of the pioneer buildings of modern architecture. It introduced the 'pilotis', columns that support the house at first floor level and also the idea of a two storey high room to give the sense of spaciousness that Le Corbusier considered a vital psychological element of freedom in housing of all types. He was to use it as a standard feature in the working families' flats in his great Unité d'Habitation.

Ritual and Refinement

In the last two chapters we have explored something of the living styles of the aristocracies of birth that ruled Europe for most of her history up to modern times. Now we turn east, where a totally different system of government prevailed and where, partly as a result, the style of living and the style of houses was also different. Imperial China, the longest-lived of all the world's great empires, was administered by a class of mandarins selected not by birth but on merit. And this was no empty phrase. Only about ten per cent of the candidates even passed the series of gruelling examinations. The subjects were the Confucian ethic of right behaviour in family and state and the classical literature of China's past. It was believed, no doubt rightly, that men who were to rule others should be learned in the traditions and customs of their people, the wisdom of the past and the correct way of behaving, so as to ensure the eternal harmony of earth and heaven. At its best, the Chinese mandarin class was a body of highly cultured professional administrators and it was their tastes which set the fashions governing Chinese art and architecture.

Social and official rank and the etiquette that went with it were of prime importance and the grades in the imperial service had special honour. There were strictly enforced regulations governing the kind of house the various officials were permitted to build. They prescribed the size of the main reception room permitted to each grade, the size of the whole building and the kind of decoration. An ordinary gentleman was not allowed a house with more than three bays. Below the third imperial grade, the main house was not to have more than five bays, while only the very highest officials were permitted decorations on the roof beams of their houses. In Japan, similar legislation even prohibited householders below a certain rank from putting a hand rail to the outer veranda of their main residence.

The house of a great Chinese gentleman was grouped round a number of courtyards. The first gave onto the main reception room, the master's library and his private drawing room. Behind this came the family courtyard, bordered by galleries which led into the rooms of his wives and concubines, the quarters of his married sons and other close relations. A central room in the main family building held the altar of the ancestors,

smaller rooms were used for storage. A third courtyard with a well was ringed by the kitchens, quarters for the maidservants and store rooms. In large establishments, guest rooms were provided round a fourth court. Several generations of a family lived in the same household, which with servants constituted a sizeable community. The main building always faced south, though, as we saw in chapter one, the actual site was

Left The garden of the seventeenth-century Cho Cheng Yuan house in Soochow is covered with water over more than half its area; notice also the winding path and the circular opening in the pavilion. *Below* The Moon Gate in the same garden in an undulating wall which imitates the waves of the sea. *Bottom* Vistas through fretwork screens were a vital element in the Chinese idea of the garden.

usually determined by the aid of diviners and astrologers.

The Chinese model of numerous single-storey dwellings and apartments grouped round courtyards, more like a Roman villa than the multi-storey buildings of Europe, was followed in Japan. In the imperial capital, the greater nobles were given plots of land, varying in size according to the noble's rank, around the palace area. The main dwelling, called the *shinden*, faced south onto a three-sided courtyard. East and west it was flanked by lesser dwellings or *tainoya*, linked to it by wide covered corridors. The two other sides of the court were formed by narrow corridors ending in small pavilions. Great nobles often built additional quarters behind the main range of *shinden* and *tainoya*, while men of lesser rank might be prohibited by law from having all the units.

Wood was the traditional building material in Japan. It was readily available, comparatively easy to work and, in an earthquake zone, less dangerous than stone. However, the main uprights were usually raised clear of the earth on stone bases to prevent rotting. Even so the timbers had to be replaced from time to time, so that the historic buildings that survive today are often the result of several reconstructions through the centuries.

Inside, a Japanese house is sparse and formal. Not only is it refreshingly free from the clutter of bric-à-brac and objets d'art that the Westerner has always gathered around him, it is also very lightly furnished. In common with many oriental cultures, the Japanese treat the floor as a common surface for activities which in the west are catered for by special pieces of furniture. Chairs are virtually unknown and beds, where they occur, are of the simplest. Consequently, the floors of a Japanese house are warm, colourful and comfortable. They are covered with heavy mats called *tatami*, about six foot by three, often in a restful green-yellow colour. Shoes are left outside and special slippers worn so that the *tatami* are not soiled with mud. At night, bed rolls are spread on the floor while low tables and arm rests can also be removed when not in use. The overall impression is of the simple geometry of the design of the walls and ceiling. The room is designed to be viewed from the eye level of someone sitting on the floor. The dimensions of the *tatami* provide the basic unit for the proportions, the pillars are spaced the length of a *tatami* apart. The lintels of the openings are six foot above floor level and this line is continued by a moulding around the room, so that whatever its size it presents familiar and balanced lines.

Another main difference between a Japanese and a European house interior is that while the space of the house can be divided into various rooms, they have interchangeable functions. Moveable partitions of wood and heavy glazed paper take the place of fixed walls so that it is easy to throw a number of smaller rooms into one or even, during the heat of the summer, to remove sections of the outer walls so that the rooms give directly onto the veranda or into the garden. Altogether, the Japanese domestic interior offers a remarkable combination of formality in design and versatility in use that has influenced modern western ideas on decor and house planning.

The owners of such houses cultivated, sometimes to an exaggerated degree, the fine arts of civilised living. Medieval Japan was a turbulent society, and reading the novels of the high medieval period gives one the feeling that the stiff formality of court and high life was devised almost consciously to shackle unruly and destructive passions. Ladies were allowed to talk to their male visitors, even their recognised fiancé, only when divided from him by a light screen and in the company of a duenna.

The calm faith of Buddhism, competing with the native shinto cults and at odds with the fiery temperament of the people, reached Japan *via* China in the sixth century. Still later, the esoteric Chinese cult of *chan* Bhuddism was transformed on Japanese soil into *zen*. At first the preserve of the religious, it gradually imposed new refinements on the attitudes expected of anyone posing as a gentleman. Among its most remarkable offshoots was the elaborate ritual that came to surround the taking of tea. The focus of social intercourse, this tea ceremony came to be defined in learned, almost mystical, treatises.

Pitie — this would look lovely in back of the Patio if you aren't addicted to NIGHT mares — HA!

Opposite page A general view of the north side of the Shokintei, built in Kyoto, Japan, in 1624. The promontory of shingle in the foreground and the rocks in the garden are an important aesthetic element and are carefully laid out. *Left* Hikone castle Japan. Despite its picturesque appearance it was a strong position and the heavy masonry base was a strong defensive feature. *Above* The Han Shan Ssu Temple at Soochow.

From the sixth century, a house with any pretensions had a tea house (*chashitsu*) with a low entrance which forced the visitor into a humble kneeling posture as he came to take part in the ceremony. Convention established that the *chashitsu* should be set apart from the main dwelling and approached over a path through a small garden, called the Dewy Path, symbolising the first break with the everyday world. The utensils of this tea ceremony, like *zen* itself a Chinese import, were handled with respect and devotion.

Many other features of Japanese house design can be traced to the influence of *zen* ideas. The *tokonoma*, a development from the altar in a priest's house, is today often the focus of the main room, where a long low table stands beneath a painting. The priest's *shoin* was a windowed study alcove built out into the veranda and it, too, was introduced into the main room of laymen's houses as a suggestion of scholarly retreat. Finally, the priest's storage cabinet for sacred scrolls became an alcove called the *tana*. Even the decorative use of flowers, found in many cultures, had in Japan semi-religious overtones deriving from *zen*. Today, the Japanese art of flower arranging has become widely known and practised in the West. The Japanese house interior was designed to provide the sympathetic atmosphere for meditation and calm communion. The same theme of meditation and calculated effect is found in the gardens of Japan and China.

Many a Chinese court official, enmeshed in the routine of administration, dreamed of an ideal life, spent communing with nature in a remote cabin in the mountains. A few revered scholar hermits did retire from the world like this and were treated with envious deference by more practical men. 'The herb path covered with red moss. The mountain window filled with pale blue sky. My friend I envy you . . .', so wrote a nostalgic city poet of the eighth century. But for him and most like him such dreams were left for the years of retirement. In the year 1559, a mandarin of the Office of Cults in Peking was looking forward to his retirement with enthusiasm:

To the west of my house there used to be a vegetable garden, fields and trees. . . . being faced with a certain period of leisure, I gathered a number of rocks and asked some workmen to arrange them to my liking. I dug a pool, built a pavilion and planted bamboos . . . I was twenty years in building this garden . . . There is a door in the west side which has carved over it, 'Beauty enters by degrees.'

Opposite top The Moon Door in the Cho Cheng Yuan House, Soochow. *Opposite bottom* A pond and pavillions of the Li Yuan garden built in the sixteenth century in Soochow. *Left* The rustic character of this garden pavillion and the path that runs along under the eaves, was a carefully contrived effect. *Below* a long view in the garden at Soochow.

In oriental gardens the placing of stones was a subtle and vital art. *Bottom* Exotically shaped rocks were mounted, as treasured objects of contemplation.

The garden was a place to encounter nature in an idealised form. The elements that went to make it, rocks, flowers, trees and above all water, were rich in symbolism. The skilled gardener, like the skilled landscape-painter, had to bring out this symbolism of the natural world and make an environment that encouraged study and reflection.

Rocks held a particularly honoured place. The strangely shaped mountains of their landscape impressed the Chinese as symbols of stability, and rocks were seen as the microcosm of a mystic world. Ones of specially refined or fantastic shapes fetched high prices at auction. They were set on pedestals or against curving white walls and were the subject of poems and scroll paintings. Every ornamental tree–apricot, plum or peach–also had its meaning. The gnarled pine was the symbol of long life and faithfulness, the tall bamboo with its suppleness and strength, was a parable of wisdom, bowing to the storm but remaining true to itself. The mandarin Po Chü-i, describes a bamboo grove in one of his poems:

I am not suited for service in a country town:
At my closed door autumn grasses grow.
What could I do to ease a rustic heart?
I planted bamboos, more than a hundred shoots.
When I see their beauty, as they grow by the
    stream-side,
I feel again as though I lived in the hills.

To prepare for himself the inspiration of these rustic reflections must have taken Po Chü-i many long hours of careful thought and design. The planting of such a bamboo grove was not a haphazard affair. Every shoot had its selected place, and often famous artists were called in to advise on the layout.

The heart of a Chinese garden was water and the site was often determined by its availability. The garden has to be a poem of light and shadow, and the glint and reflections of rivulets, waterfalls and lakes were the magical element that brought it alive. Streams and ponds were designed in sinuous curves so that from no one vantage point could one see both their beginning and their end. The pulsating light reflected from their surfaces dissolved the forms of the garden and enveloped them in an air of mystery.

Accustomed in his official life to etiquette and bureaucratic formality, the Chinese mandarin banished symmetry from his garden retreat. Chinese town gardens were larger than those in the west and were designed as an extension of the house. Although surrounded by the bustle of the city, it was intended to seem like a secret glade in some vast dream landscape, where the stroller could follow his every whim. Winding paths and unexpected openings lead to a succession of separate vistas and retreats: to summer houses, little libraries, rooms for music, rooms for study and rooms for the cultivation of the tea ceremony. The human world and the natural world were felt to share a deep communion and it was the job of the gardener, as of the landscape painter, to interpret this. Garden design also owed much to the retreats built for themselves by early taoist monks. They, so to speak, were the professionals of the contemplative way, and the mandarins of the city hoped by following their example to find something of their secret of spiritual peace.

In contrast to the eastern enthusiasm for natural objects the West has until recently tended to see shapes and stories in natural forms. Here is a magnificent example of sculpture in living rock from Bomarzo, Italy.

why don't you put one of these where your front door is?

During the late seventeenth and eighteenth centuries, European fashions were heavily coloured by the intellectual interest in things Chinese. While the Electors of Saxony were subsidising the breaking of the age-long secret of porcelain manufacture in their factory at Meissen, the French philosopher Voltaire was enviously discovering that in the east the ideal of a state ruled by philosophers had been realised. Chinese ideas of house and garden, often misunderstood, changed the emphasis in European garden design. We have seen how many eighteenth-century European houses had 'Chinese' pavilions in their grounds and the great movement of English landscape garden architecture traces some of its inspiration to the east. The formal and geometrical designs of the seventeenth century gave place to more naturalistic compositions. But while the Chinese ideal had been to recreate an artificial and idealised environment where one could meditate on the mystical bonds that knit man into the natural world, the English gentleman sought to tame that world. Surveying his landscaped park, with its spreading vistas of spacious prosperity, the western nobleman did not view himself as part of the natural world. On the contrary, comfortably isolated from is blustery reality, he prided himself on being its proprietor.

We find a very different interpretation of the Chinese ideal in the gardens of Japan, there it becomes still more abstract. Gone is the Chinese love of water with its subtle and shimmering effects. Instead we find the immobility of sand, raked into wave patterns and stiffened into silent, frozen waterfalls. The Daisenin Garden, in the Daitokuji Temple at Kyoto, is considered by the Japanese to be one of the greatest achievements of the garden art. Laid out in the sixteenth century, its ultimate inspiration comes from Chinese landscape paintings of some three hundred years earlier, reinterpreted by Japanese artists. Rocks and sand are sensitively used to create the impression of streams and cascades and waterside scenes. A decade or so earlier, a still more abstract effect had been achieved at the garden of the Ryoanji zen temple, also in Kyoto.

In an oblong of coarse white sand are set a mere fifteen rocks in groups of two, three and five. The garden may only be viewed from a veranda-like platform round part of two of its sides. It is the purest expression of zen mysticism in the art of the garden and has puzzled generations of interpreters. Perhaps the most fascinating enigma is the one stone that cannot be seen from any position on the viewing platform.

Above Lady Hester Stanhope entertaining guests. *Below* The garden of the Ryoanji temple in Kyoto, Japan, pictured from the viewing platform.

The west has been importing luxuries from the orient at least since the time of Rome. When the European went to live in alien civilisations, he generally tried to set up a replica of his own way of life. However, if only because the style of housing evolved in these ancient cultures was perfectly adapted to the climate, he was bound to adopt some of its conventions. The extended single-storey dwelling of Bengal, has given a word to the English language. The bungalow, now so familiar in British and American suburbia takes its name from the Indian word *Bangla,* literally 'of Bengal'. Originally a peasant dwelling, it was surrounded with wide verandas offering shade from the sun and protection against the rains in the monsoon season. It had few rooms, large window and door openings to promote a maximum of cross draughts, and a high roof.

Many of the English in India, impressed by the high civilisation that they found there, even adopted customs of dress and social behaviour. It was not only diplomatic, it was also comfortable and a fascinating new kind of luxury. Contemporary paintings show British officers sitting cross-legged on rich carpets and enjoying a cool smoke from a hookah as they watch entertainments laid on in their honour by their Indian hosts. Others wore Indian dress even when they entertained at home. Many of their European contemporaries no doubt classed such behaviour as eccentric.

Even more eccentric was the behaviour of the nineteenth-century Lady Hester Stanhope, a noble Englishwoman who settled in the Lebanon and held court from her house for many years. The wonder of Arab and European alike, she moved with the freedom of a man in an all-male Arab society, wearing Arab costume, without the *yashmak* obligatory for Muslim women. Her house was furnished throughout in Arabian style and she entertained her guests sitting cross-legged on a low divan and smoking a hookah.

However, most Europeans kept to their own traditions and their houses showed little influence of Indian architecture. Country residences and the homes of lesser European officials were sometimes in the style of the Indian house, notably the bungalow, but in large mansions the architecture

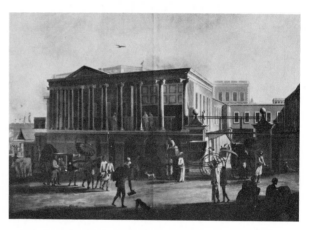

Above The presence of the Europeans in India was proclaimed by their houses. *Below* Officers of the British East India Company enjoyed the luxurious life of the East.

Right Behind the cascade is the casino of the Villa Farnese, Caprarola. *Below* The Palazzo Contarini del Bovolo in Venice. The magnificent staircase served a very practical purpose being the only connecting link between the different floors. Since the ground floor was usually occupied by tradesmen and the top floors by poor lodgers, the family on the middle floor had to protect its privacy as best it could. *Opposite* The Amber Palace, India. The formal gardens of this Moslem mansion have surprising similarities of mood with the geometric designs of Italian Renaissance gardens.

The Italy of the Renaissance and for centuries to come, was divided between a number of principalities and powers. They range from small territories like that of the dukes of Urbino to the rich and dazzling might of Venice whose maritime empire stretched down the Adriatic to the Aegean sea. It was in these flourishing and independent states that the merchant class of Europe first came into its own. In the great northern kingdom of France, even in the seventeenth century, the high road to riches and prestige still lay through the offices of the royal court. Formal salaries were not over large but the opportunities open to officers of state to line their own pockets out of the revenues of their departments were immense. In fact they constituted the chief attraction of the royal service to most ambitious men. The houses we turn to all belong to this century and were all built on this kind of money. Today they appear as part of a proud national heritage, but even when they were built they were seen by some as the fruits of corruption.

Homes in the New World

The house as such was virtually unknown to the inhabitants of northern America before the coming of the white man. In chapter two we saw something of the remarkable snow houses designed by the Eskimos of the frozen North. In the southwest, the villages of the Pueblo Indians consisted of solid and permanent earth-and-timber structures, but in the Great Central Plains and the eastern woodlands the standard dwellings were more tentlike. The wigwam of the Algonquin peoples was a more or less permanent conical or domed structure covered with squares of bark, reed mats or thatch. The smaller wigwams housed single families, but larger examples were communal dwellings. A similar type is the wikiup of the peoples of Arizona, Utah, Idaho and California. It consists of a framework of arched poles covered again with brushwood, bark rushes or mats. The tepee, or tipi, of the tribes of the Great Plains, such as the Sioux and the Blackfoot, was different from the wigwam – it was portable as befitted the dwelling of a nomadic people. It was made from a frame of poles covered with tightly stretched skins, usually buffalo hide, and despite its temporary nature offered good protection against the weather. It was so adaptable to the conditions of life on the prairie that it was used by General Henry Sibley as the model for the design of the tents for his army in campaigns against the Sioux themselves.

The very first English settlers around Jamestown, Virginia, in the early years of the seventeenth century followed the example of the original inhabitants in home building. Their 'English wigwams', consisted of tunnel-shaped frames of wood over a trench of about a foot or two deep, covered with bark. Other equally primitive dwellings were roofed with turf but very early the European introduced the fireplace to his home and by the 1640s an observer noted joyfully: 'The Lord has been pleased to transform all the tents, huts and hovels which the English lived in when they arrived into well-built houses, many of them furnished also.'

The magnificent Lee family mansion, Stratford Hall, Va., built in the early years of the eighteenth century.

These houses were of the half-timbered type. A wooden frame was filled in with brush-wood and branches and then sealed with mud. This type was long common in England, as we saw in the case of John Hathaway's house at Shottery. In the Midlands the daub was left open to the weather, but in the east where the bleak wind sweeps across the flat Fen country, the walls were covered with clap-boarding, overlapping boards. This style was also adopted in New England, no doubt for added protection against the hard winters.

At first, the average American's house was a one-room affair. Folding beds and collapsible tables made it possible to use the single hall for all living functions, and these ingenious pieces of furniture continued long in favour. Floors of wide rough beams were uncovered, except, perhaps, for 'crumb cloths' under the table to make cleaning up easier – carpets were rarely seen and were more often used as table coverings or preserved as valuable objets d'art. Early colonial America was a poor if a hardy society. Even bowls and platters were made of wood, and they remained so well into the eighteenth century in all but the richest houses, because porcelain had to be imported from across the Atlantic. Even when well-to-do households could afford to commission pewter ware from local craftsmen this often had a short life, being melted down for the metals it contained if the family fell on hard times.

In the course of time, the settler's house developed. An entrance porch was soon added while a staircase led up beside the chimney to a sleeping loft above the main room which was called the 'keeping room'. Better-off families began building two-room dwellings, one room at ground level on either side of the chimney, which now had two back-to-back fireplaces. The additional room, called the parlour, tended to be kept for receiving important visitors or for special occasions. Within a generation, two rooms was the standard and the larger houses came to boast added accommodation at the back of the house, usually under a lean-to, extended from the roof rafters, consisting of small low-roofed rooms.

Even at this time, important people in a 'New England' village community had sizeable two-storey dwellings where the loft under the roof provided a sort of third storey for storage or

Wall paintings were a common form of decoration from the middle ages through to the eighteenth century. The magnificent Heaven Room at Burghley House, England (page 63) is a fine example of the later stage of the art. *Opposite top* An early example of wall painting from the medieval Palazzo Davanzati, Florence. *Opposite bottom* The gardens of the Villa d'Este, the most magnificent, perhaps, among the many magnificent gardens in Italy. *Above* The superb Hall of the Annals at the Villa Farnese by the Zuccaro brothers. From floor to ceiling the room is lined with the story of the family of the builder of the villa. *Left* A glimpse of the cascade in the gardens of the Villa Farnese, Caprarola.

Eighteenth-century America witnessed the building of many splendid mansions as the colonists increased in wealth and sophistication. Naturally, the architecture remained largely indebted to contemporary European styles, but for all that a place like Stratford Hall, built in the late 1720s by Thomas Lee, shows immense confidence of design. Lee descended from a family that had been loyal to the Royalist cause during the English Civil War. Coming to America, the family had built its fortune on tobacco and were important figures in the commonwealth of Virginia, but they did not lose sight at once of their English connections and Stratford Hall, with its 'H' plan and great hall, reflect the impressions that Lee brought back with him from a visit to the old country. However, in the way in which he used the brick of which the house at Stratford is built, the architect achieved a marked originality of effect. The fact that the main rooms are on the first floor, the *piano nobile* of the Italian Renaissance villa, makes one wonder whether Lee had also visited Robert Adam's masterpiece for Sir Francis Child at Osterley Park.

In 1730 the Lee family was important in Virginia. In the next generation it became important throughout America. Thomas's son was Richard Henry Lee, one of the leading statesmen during the War of Independence, but the most famous member of the line, also born at Stratford Hall, was the great Confederate general, Robert E. Lee. Since 1935, this home of a great family of distinguished southerners has been revered as a national shrine and today the estate around the house is run as a type of museum where the activities of a plantation of former times, hand-weaving and spinning and the curing of hams, are still practised.

America's most famous mansion is, of course, the White House, designed by the Irish-born architect James Hoban. The site was chosen by President Washington and he took the closest interest in the progress of the building, described on the plans as a 'palace'. But Washington never lived there. It was finished only in 1799, the year of his death, and was inaugurated as the presidential residence by President John Adams.

Washington's home, from the age of fifteen in 1747 until his death, was Mount Vernon, overlooking the Potomac River, near Alexandria, Va. The house had been built in 1743 by his half-brother Lawrence who had served under Admiral Vernon in the British Navy and named the house after him. After his brother's death in 1752, young George inherited the house. Subsequently

he commissioned alterations that were not completed when he died. The mansion, built of timber, shows the characteristic lines of a Georgian house and is fronted by a handsome columned portico. It stands in fine gardens with spreading lawns and has been restored, following detailed notes left by Washington himself, under the auspices of the Mount Vernon Ladies' Association which purchased the property in 1860 and remains its custodian. The most important national shrine, Mount Vernon houses family relics and much of the original furniture. In fact, thanks to the careful reconstruction of duplicate pieces, the interior of the house is much as it was in the lifetime of the great statesman. In the grounds stands the tomb, built in the 1830s, with the sarcophagi of George and Martha Washington and the bodies of other members of the family.

Thomas Jefferson, third president of the United States and prime author of the Declaration of Independence, stands high among the founding fathers of modern America. He was a man of varied talents, for he was the architect of the mansion at Monticello near Charlottesville, which was to be his home until his death. Work began in 1770. The style was in the tradition of the Palladian revival, not long established in Europe and then almost unknown in the US. The house is brick built with a handsome stone porch and white balustrades at roof level. It is cruciform with semi-octagonal bays at the end of each wing. The effect is of grace, strength and originality. The actual building was done by Jefferson's black artisan slaves and the materials, from the timber to the very nails, were prepared on his estate. After his death, the estate passed to his daughter but she, unable to maintain the place, sold it. The new owner bequeathed it to the nation but the will was contested successfully by his heirs and it was not until 1923 that it returned to the national heritage. Bought by the Thomas Jefferson Memorial Foundation, it was extensively restored and has been open to the public since 1954.

Top The handsome porch of Monticello, near Charlottesville, Va., the home that Thomas Jefferson designed for himself. Its originality, confidence and stylishness, make it one of the finest houses of the eighteenth century.
Bottom left A dining alcove at Monticello.
Bottom right Interior of the great house at Mount Pleasant, Philadelphia.

A beautiful view of the gardens at
Vaux-le-Vicomte through the window of a
handsome painted wood panelled room.

The Library at Vaux-le-Vicomte now furnished
with the comfortable upholstery of the
nineteenth and twentieth centuries.

The new century, to be one of the most exciting in the history of architecture, opened with a house that has been called the 'crowning achievement of the Craftsman Movement'. That movement, inspired by the work of William Morris in England, approached natural materials with the kind of loving care of the medieval craftsman and had little in common with the approach of modern machine-age designers. The house, built in Pasadena, Calif. in 1909, was designed by the architects Charles and Henry Greene for David Gamble, a director of the Cincinatti-based firm of Proctor & Gamble, as a winter house. The last member of the original owners died in 1942 and the house is now in the care of the University of Southern California. Yet distant cousins of the family occasionally overnight here so that this monument of one of the great moments in American architecture still breathes the atmosphere of a family home. The house is constructed largely of wood by a pair of designers backed up by talented local craftsmen.

A dozen years later, the Austrian-born architect Rudolf Schindler built a house for himself and his friend Clyde Chase on Sunset Boulevard which is now being hailed as one of the most original in modern architecture. Making use of concrete at a time when it was hardly accepted as a housing material in America, and in a way that was matched only by Le Corbusier, Schindler developed a flexible environment fully integrated with its landscape in which glass-sided rooms alternate with open roofed courtyards.

From the very beginning of the century, America had a world-leading architect in Frank Lloyd Wright. Of his more than one thousand buildings, most are suburban houses; few architects have designed with more success for the conditions of twentieth-century living.

In the early 1900s, around Chicago, Ill., he built a number of what he called 'Prairie' houses because they were long and low and hugged the land. They were not simply æsthetic masterpieces, nor simply among the most important buildings of the twentieth century, they were also magnificent places for living in. The brilliant, intuitive arrangement of the rooms and the spaces within the house give full play to the conflicting desires of modern man for intimacy, privacy and freedom of movement. One of the most famous of these houses is the Robie House in Chicago. Built as early as 1909, it incorporated the garage as part of the overall plan and was one of the first to do so. It is now preserved as an historic building, one that heralded Wright's influence in Europe after 1910.

Brought up on a farm, Wright had a deep respect for the land and described his architecture as 'organic', to indicate that each house should as far as possible grow out of its site. In the middle of the machine age, he proclaimed a doctrine that took man back to his beginnings when his home was quite literally a part of the landscape.

Nowhere is Wright's sense of landscape more dramatically expressed than in his famous house for Edgar Kaufmann at Bear Run, Penn., built in 1935–37. It stands among woods on a steep and rocky site and the end of the main room, with a terrace above, overhangs a waterfall. As the house climbs the hillside, one side has access points to the rising ground levels, while the other offers romantic views from its terraces. A suspended stairway leads down from a hatch in the living room to the waterfall and the link between man, his home and nature is complete. The daring design would have been inconceivable without modern techniques and materials, and could not have been realised without the backing of a wealthy client. But for all that Falling Water is imbued with the simple love of nature that was the foundation of the architect's creed.

Edgar Kaufmann also had a second house built for himself. This was a winter house commissioned from the architect Richard Neutra. The site was sensational and so were the solutions that the architect found. The house was set on the edge of the California Desert at Palm Springs and the strong horizontals of its roofs and patios contrast beautifully with the rugged landscape of mountains behind. It was a place of luxury in an arid setting. Glass was used freely for walls which could even be slid bodily back to open the interior to the courtyard spaces and the landscape. The climate is harsh, and unless the house were kept in constant occupancy the desert sands drift back, despite the sophisticated controls that Neutra built into his design. Homes like this are the modern equivalent of the aristocratic palaces of an earlier age. They are the homes of a modern ruling class of wealth, and while the life-style they are designed for is entirely different, being relaxed and informal as well as elegant, they are clearly the homes of privilege. Like any Renaissance villa, the Kaufmann Desert House has extensive servants' quarters. Earlier the wealthy had had more traditional ideas of what a great man's house should look like. The superb Vanderbilt estate at Asheville, NC, is a fine example. The extremes of grandiose display, however, must surely have been reached in the fantastic castle groaning with its still more fantastic collection of

Top The classic statement of the modern domestic style which Frank Lloyd Wright achieved in his Robie House, Chicago (1909) was an important moment in modern architecture. *Above* The Lovell Beach House, built at Newport Beach in 1925–26 by Rudolph Schindler (d. 1953) who has been described as 'the least understood and least appreciated of the pioneers of modern American architecture.'

works of art that William Randolph Hearst built for himself at San Simeon, Calif. It inspired a film set in Orson Welles's famous *Citizen Kane* and in truth it seems more like a film set than a real building.

American house design in the twentieth century covers the whole exciting range of modern architecture. At the other extreme from the imitative extravagances of San Simeon is the innovatory Dymaxion House, designed by R. Buckminster Fuller in the 1920s. The word 'dymaxion' is his own coinage to sum up his principle of the maximum output for the minimum input of energy and materials, and Fuller's life-long passion has been to see the world's resources deployed to the greatest possible advantage for the whole population of the earth. The Dymaxion House was designed as a single, cheap and self-contained unit that could be delivered anywhere by air. It provided all the necessary services and was costed so that, given the right diversion of industry and resources, the task of building adequate homes for all who wanted them could be realised. It was a marvellous dream and one that could be realised far more easily than sending men to the moon, but, of course, it remains a dream.

The Château de Valençay, France, where the
great nineteenth century statesman Talleyrand
lived.

An interior in the Hôtel Lambert, Paris. For generations the great house was derelict or being used for storage and similar purposes. It has been carefully restored and the solid mid-seventeenth century French furniture restores the air of opulent and solid grandeur.

Modernism of another kind was announced by Philip Johnson in his Glass House at New Canaan, Conn., in 1949. Standing among trees and illuminated at night to give a dramatic and simple abstract design, the stark, delicately calculated lines of this glass and metal box provide a geometry for living that is fascinating, if also cold and exposed. The imagination of Bruce Goff has turned to richer fantasies. He produces houses that sometimes look like space domes designed for moon dwellers or for elves or 'Middle Earth' rather than homes for ordinary earthmen. The very names (one is called 'Residence for a Lover of Plants') indicate the searching and ingenious imagination of this inventive architect. Buildings like this show how difficult is the search if we are looking to define a 'house'. From the simple cruck house to the snailshells of Bruce Goff seems like a journey from one planet to another. Where the peasant's hut stands foursquare against its environment to keep out the weather as best it can, the aim of many modern house architects is to bring the landscape environment into the closest possible connection with the living area. Techniques, materials and the whole pattern of industrialised living have given us such mastery over nature that our problem is no longer how much to keep her at bay, but rather how to bring ourselves back into harmony with her. Advanced modern houses reflect this need in modern man, as homes throughout the ages have embodied the ideas and ideals of their builders.

Two views of the Glass House, New Canaan, Conn., designed by Philip Johnson in 1949.